UNLEASH YOUR LEADER

HOW TO WIN IN BUSINESS

UNLEASH YOUR LEADER

HOW TO WIN IN BUSINESS

EMMANUEL GOBILLOT
and KATHERINE THOMAS

Urbane
BUSINESS

urbanepublications.com

First published in Great Britain in 2019
by Urbane Publications Ltd
Suite 3, Brown Europe House, 33/34 Gleaming Wood Drive,
Chatham, Kent ME5 8RZ
Copyright © Emmanuel Gobillot and Katherine Thomas

A CIP catalogue record for this book is available
from the British Library.

ISBN 978-1-912666-19-5
MOBI 978-1-912666-20-1

Design and Typeset by Michelle Morgan

Cover by Julie Martin

Printed and bound by 4edge Limited, UK

Urbane
BUSINESS
urbanepublications.com

On ne choisit pas sa famille mais on choisit ses amis.
A Nathalie Gobillot, ma soeur et meilleure amie.

To my father Professor Edward Thomas.
After your own book dedication to me, over forty
years ago, finally I have the opportunity to return the
compliment!

TABLE OF CONTENTS ⋆

So you want to be a leader …

Three steps to win the top spot

Step 3 – STEADFAST IMPACT -
Changing your impact whilst staying intact

ACKNOWLEDGEMENTS *

Neither of us has ever co-written a book before. One thing we knew when we started though was that we wanted to use the singular voice. We felt that using the plural throughout would be clumsy and sound somehow pretentious.

The problem with this choice however is that it automatically conveys the sense that this is the work of one person alone. It hides the contributions of the hundreds of people who, through conversations, interactions or more formal interviews, have given shape to this book.

In fact, over 200 people have contributed their thoughts and ideas to our research. That number makes it impractical to name them all, but we owe them a huge debt of gratitude for their input.

There are, however, two organizations in particular that set us forth on the journey that would eventually become this book.

First, we must thank the executive team of Coloplast, Lars Rasmussen, President and CEO, Anders Lonning-Skovgaard, EVP & CFO, Kristian Villumsen, EVP Chronic Care and Allan Rasmussen, EVP Global Operations for challenging us to articulate the unique requirements of executive transitions under the direction of Thomas Alsbjerg, VP Corporate HR and the guidance of Lea Goldin Green Pein, Director of Talent and Leadership Development.

However, it was the Talent and Culture team at ANZ Bank who planted the seed in our heads that executive transitions would be something worth writing about. We must also thank the Executive team of ANZ for trusting us enough to let us interact with their senior leaders in a way that allowed us to start digging deeper into the topic. We owe a great deal to those we met at ANZ, not only for their insights, but for making our frequent 24-hour trips across the world over the last year feel like short commutes.

There are three executives who took time out of their busy schedule to test out some of the tools we advocate and provided us with thorough feedback. Our thanks therefore must go to Magnus Albertson, Head of Sales and Customer Service, Marine Andre, Liquid Innovation & Sensory Director and Thomas Paludan-Müller, Master Brewer and Director Liquid Implementation at Carlsberg Group for their invaluable insights.

Of course we could not have got here without the incredible work of the team at Urbane under the direction of Kerry Jane Lowery. Matthew Smith, Director of Publications, whose project this was, has been instrumental in Emmanuel's writing journey and the start of Katherine's. The value of his advice, challenges, support and contributions should by right earn him a mention on the front cover of this book. Any author who ever wonders what the point of publishers still is in this self-published world has clearly never met Matthew and the team.

Without the contribution of all the people above and indeed that of the many other executives we have had the pleasure of working alongside over the last few decades, this book would not exist. Any mistake however is down to us and us alone in our attempt to translate their voices.

Finally, a book cannot be on a shelf as a result of the work of its authors and publisher alone. For a book to be printed it needs potential readers so we must thank you for picking it up. Whatever brought you to this page we hope we can repay your decision with the value we aim to share.

SO YOU WANT TO BE A LEADER... ★

Who would have thought Sergeant Martin held the secret to becoming a leader?

We hated his demeanor. We couldn't stand watching him approach our sleeping quarters. We feared his put-downs. We worried every time we heard him shout our names.

As luck would have it, I wasn't the main target of his abuse. That honor was bestowed upon my fellow conscript "petiot" (a colloquial French word for child), so called because his surname was Pitiot (he wasn't the wittiest man, our Sergeant).

"Petiot" had made a very early tactical mistake. On his first day in the barracks, freshly shaven and uniformed, he had had the audacity to declare that he wanted to become an officer.

The fact that the lowest ranking Second Class Pitiot could possibly think that he could outrank a Sergeant was not something Sergeant Martin was about to let pass. So, every day, during every drill, he would delight in screaming "look at you, petiot, you'll never make a soldier, never mind an officer".

It took Pitiot more courage than any of us had (an aspiring officer's kind of courage I guess) to finally stand up to Sergeant Martin. Pushed to the limit by the endless taunts of "you will never become an officer", he finally dared to ask why.

I will always remember that day, not because of the punishment Pitiot suffered for his affront – to be honest I can't even remember what it was - but because Sergeant Martin uttered a sentence I have used many times since.

About an inch away from Pitiot's face, in a full metal jacket move, with the force of a hurricane, Sergeant Martin shouted:

"You will never become an officer, Second Class Aviator Pitiot, because you are not an officer."

Far be it for me to question Sergeant Martin's logic but that statement was either incredibly clumsy or incredibly profound. All evidence would point to clumsy, but I thought I should check.

I had to wait until after our passing out parade to do so. His task of turning us into semi acceptable soldiers now complete, Sergeant Martin relaxed enough for me to ask him. So, we went to the bar and we talked (and I paid).

I asked him why he had been so harsh on Pitiot and more precisely why he thought he would never make the grade. His answer underpins the blueprint I want to share with you on your journey to becoming a leader.

"The only way to become an officer is to be an officer. It is to do the things officers do. To speak the way officers speak. To behave the way officers behave. To do all these things so naturally that no one ever questions why you should be an officer but rather questions why you are not one already."

It is only now, some thirty years later, having studied hundreds of leaders and been lucky enough to accompany many of them on their transition to top roles that I know Sergeant Martin was right.

I also know there are three questions that must be answered for you to unleash your leader. These are the three questions we will answer together in this book.

1. **What are the unique requirements of a top leadership role?**
   This book is not about becoming a leader. It is about getting you to the top. Irrespective of your position, you must set your sights on the top job if you are to get anywhere near it. Pitiot wasn't aiming to become a petty officer. He wanted the top grade. So, if you can only be a top leader when you speak like a top leader and behave like a top leader, you need to know what the unique characteristics of a top leadership role are. I will share these with you.

2. **How should I go about meeting these?**
   You can only become a top leader if you master the strategies, tactics, habits, models and frameworks that help you fulfill these unique characteristics. I will equip you with these.

3. **How can I display my newfound leadership skills in my current role?**
   For others to ask why you are not at the top already they must see you behave like a senior leader even when your role does not require it. I will show you how to hack your day job in order to get your dream one.

My aim is to give you an insider view into the world of successful executives and share with you a blueprint to ensure that, whoever your Sergeant is, she will be compelled to ask herself why you are not a senior leader yet.

RECAP

The secret to unleashing your leader is do the things leaders do, speak the way leaders speak and behave the way leaders behave. It is to do these things so naturally that no one ever questions why you should be a senior leader, but rather questions why you are not one already.

THREE STEPS TO WIN THE TOP SPOT

1 FRAMEWORK FOR BECOMING THE IDEAL SUCCESSOR

QUESTIONS THIS CHAPTER ANSWERS

How do you know you are ready to become a senior leader?

What are the unique requirements of a top leadership role you will need to master to stand a chance of getting one?

They had to operate in the C suite.

That was the only criterion that decided who made the cut for the research that underpins this book. They could be from any sector of the economy, any industry, any geography, recognized as successful or not so successful, in fact the more variety the better, but they had to operate in the C suite.

Why? Because anyone interested in a book on how to become a leader is either or both successful and ambitious. And these attributes demand a targeted research approach.

Whichever one of success or ambition has brought you here, there is embedded in both a desire to reach your full potential as well as a fear that it may be overlooked. So, what can you do to ensure others cannot avoid spotting this?

First you need to understand the unique requirements of a senior leadership role. What is it that is unique about the role and that you, in your current one, do not have the chance to experience?

Second, given the above, how do you ensure that you create opportunities to master a response to these unique requirements in your current role in a way all can see?

But before I share with you these things that, to paraphrase Sergeant Martin, will get you to be the leader you want to become, there is something we need to clear up. There is a question you need to answer for yourself.

I am assuming, given you are reading this book that you already know the answer to the question "am I ready?" So let me rephrase it slightly "how do I know I am ready to make the transition to the top spot"?

Here is a list of what you need to know and be able to do before you are ready to attempt the transition. These are the elements you can't do without. Quite frankly you shouldn't be a leader, never mind aspire to reach the top of any organization, without them.

The non-negotiable basics

Basic #1 - You know your stuff.

This applies whatever your stuff is. If you are a marketer I expect you to know about marketing. If you are an HR person, then I expect you to know about HR.

Knowing your stuff is not enough and, in and of itself, nor is it a differentiator. But it is critical. It's your ticket to the game.

Basic #2 - You also know what you don't need to know but need an opinion on

Knowing your stuff is not the same as knowing all there is to know.

Executives have to rely on people who know more than they do. What is more, the most common cause of executive failures is when people come to believe and act as if they can do everything alone.

What is expected of a senior leader is not that she will be able to do everything but that she will have an opinion about anything.

So, if you are a marketer I expect you to know about marketing, but I don't necessarily expect you to be a data scientist. However, I do expect you to have a view on the role data plays in marketing. I also expect you, even though you're a marketer, to have a view about how big data can help your HR colleagues make better decisions on talent targeting.

I also, as it happens, expect you to know some of the best data scientists out there and I would love it if at least a few of them were willing to work for you.

Basic #3 - You are fluent in finance

Finance is the language of business and you have to be fluent in it.

And I don't mean knowing your balance sheets from your profit and loss statements. I don't mean being a spreadsheet jockey able to do a dance on a pivot table.

I mean knowing how cash flows through the system. I mean knowing your way around an analyst note. I mean understanding how your business is valued.[1]

If you happen to work in the not for profit sector or in a governmental agency this also applies to you. You may need to replace analysts' notes with policy papers or funding agencies' news, but you still need to speak finance.

Basic #4 – People want to work with you

I am assuming you know your IQ from your EQ (and if you don't know what the initials mean you had better find out). I take it as read that you are versatile in terms of the styles you use. I assume people want to follow you - even when they don't have to.

This is not a book about basic leadership principles, but I expect you to have read at least one.

Needless to say, the four assumptions above are not the only things you need to succeed. This is a book for people who are looking for the corner office not the slightly bigger cubicle. So, the four basics above are the minimal requirements.

I could name many more. There is cultural awareness. You want a pinch of political savvy. It would be helpful to throw in a cup of

----

1. There are two books I can recommend that will be of help to understand the fundamentals of business finance if you are not a finance person (and indeed there is a third you should read if you are a finance person). For a short and to the point volume on what you need to know there is no better title than 'What the CEO Wants You to Know' by Ram Sharan. It has been in print for a while which in my book is a good thing. I would also recommend that you read 'Value: The Four Cornerstones of Corporate Finance" by McKinsey & Company Inc. It will be a good way to test your understanding of how people in the finance community (and by extension Senior Executives) look at a business. At the very least it will help you understand what's in the mind of a McKinsey person and given many CEOs either have been McKinsey people, or get calls from them regularly, that should be helpful too! If you happen to be a finance person then a must read (if you haven't already) is the bigger version of the one above called 'Valuation: Measuring and Managing the Value of Companies'. If you can't be bothered with any of the above then do me a favour. Google "McKinsey on valuation" and watch the YouTube video. That's the least you can do to find out if you know enough!

communication and a spoonful of negotiation skills.

Every book and article you read, video you watch and podcast you listen to will give you some other ingredient.

They are probably right, and it would be great to have them all.

That being said, your time is limited and focus is key.

So, the above four are your starting point. The "non-negotiables" are just that - non-negotiable. You have to be honest with yourself when you assess your readiness to progress. Go back to the basics before you attempt to move on or you'll not only be wasting your time and energy, but you will potentially damage your credibility in a way that will be hard to recover from.

Now let's get back to our purpose here. Let's focus on what is unique about top leadership roles.

The unique requirements of a senior leadership role

As you would guess when you ask top executives "what is unique about your role?" and "what do you wish you had known before taking this on?" as we did for our research, you get a myriad of answers.

They range from the vague "I am ultimately the one in charge" to the highly specific "I wish I had known just how much trouble the business was in".

Given some answers are more helpful than others, when sifting through our research data, we looked for two specific characteristics.

1. What were the answers that were shared across the respondent group irrespective of demographics (including geography, industry etc.)?

2. What were the answers that were shared irrespective of experience and performance (i.e. what were the things even the most experienced and successful incumbents wish they had known)?

Using these two criteria to isolate the data painted a very clear picture. That picture is our blueprint.

What is unique about a top leadership role is the significant ramp up of three elements – Perspective, Agility and Impact. To reflect what successful executives do we call the three attributes Boundless Perspective, Vertical Agility and Steadfast Impact.

If you want to make the transition from where you are now to become a credible executive, you need to master all three. Let's take each in turn in this chapter before we dive deeper into what you need to do to master them.

BOUNDLESS PERSPECTIVE

This dimension is all about the absence of boundaries.

We know that, from customers to community leaders via analysts and politicians, the stakeholder community senior leaders have to deal with is vast.

To be successful we need to be able to scan our environment from the broadest perspective and bring the outside in. We need to see the wood from the trees whilst operating at a speed where everything is blurred. We need to have networks that span way beyond what we would normally consider useful to unearth value others seldom see. Boundless perspective is about having the curiosity to search, the willingness to hear, the skill to combine and the courage to rise above narrow-minded considerations to bring value to the business by challenging received wisdom.

VERTICAL AGILITY

Almost without exception the leaders we interviewed for our research underestimated the significant ramp up in the complexity, breadth, time pressure, noise etc. that comes with making decisions at a C-suite level.

All of them described the challenges that come with running a business whilst at the same time trying to change and adapt it.

Success requires agility both in thinking and acting. The ability to roll your sleeves up operationally at the same time as making decisions strategically can catch out even the most seasoned professional. It is not just being able to do both. Most of you have mastered that already. It is being able to do both at once and at speed that differentiates.

You need filters to simplify whilst being mindful not to be derailed by being overly simplistic. You need some plans that you hold firm, along with others that you willingly let go as quickly as changes in the environment demand.

If you ever found yourself declaiming the focus on short term results that deprives us of long-term opportunities, or caught yourself musing on the advantages of being global versus local, or bemoaned the absence of strategic thinking that compromised operational excellence, you had better be able to put aside such dichotomies quickly. At executive level the only possible answer to any dilemma is summed up in two words: "both" and "now".

STEADFAST IMPACT

This dimension refers to the unlikely and seemingly paradoxical marriage of consistency and differentiation.

It is about recognizing that the lens you are under as a leader is microscopic. Everything you say and do is watched and analyzed whilst everything you think is extrapolated from your words and deeds. Some people need to know you are both authentic and consistent. Others will seek to prove you are neither.

You need to appeal to multiple constituencies by being flexible enough to adapt your message (differentiation) without ever compromising on what you hold to be true (consistency), but always be willing to question your thinking.

Learning to manage this level of scrutiny is key. Seeking counsel to understand and knowing when to step back and forward is necessary. Knowing your core and having the courage to make decisions based on this without falling prey to hubris or populism is critical.

Being a senior executive also means being a leader of leaders. It is about understanding that organizations and the people who inhabit them are fundamentally flawed and dysfunctional. We all are!

Where some see the need for team building, our blueprint demands the need for impact. It dictates that you recognize the dysfunctions around you and learn to manage them, knowing that they will seldom be eradicated.

I am, of course, also aware that once you add the list of non-negotiable basics I went through earlier to these three unique characteristics of leadership roles, our blueprint sounds optimistically delusional. The reality though is that mastering these three steps to land the top job is a deliberate act. It is a matter of diligence and discipline in the application of a number of habits.

In the remainder of this book I will share with you the practices developed by the leaders who stood out in our research as masters of each of these elements. I will deconstruct what they do and together we will find ways to integrate these elements into your current routines and practices.

There is one more thing we need to cover before we go there though. To be successful in applying any of the practices I will share with you, you will first need to have the right attitude, both in how you approach the challenge of doing something new, but also in how you manage your impact on others as you grow.

Adopt the wrong mindset and you will more than likely fall behind in your efforts to move forward. The good news is that it is possible to predict, with quite a high degree of accuracy, who will succeed and who will fail. Let me share with you the attitude that will ensure you start on the right foot as you take the three steps.

RECAP

There are four basic skills you need to have before you can even think of making it to the top.

Basic #1 - You know your stuff.
Basic #2 - You also know what you don't need to know but on which you need an opinion.
Basic #3 - You are fluent in finance.
Basic #4 – People want to work with you.

Once you have mastered these four you are ready to tackle the three unique characteristics of executive roles.

BOUNDLESS PERSPECTIVE

- The need to scan and understand the environment from the broadest perspective in order to identify the external forces that matter.
- The ability to establish networks of value within and beyond organiational boundaries to identify and leverage how value is created.

VERTICAL AGILITY

- The ability to work effectively for both the long-term and in the moment – oscillating between strategy formulation and execution as required.
- The need to resolve dilemmas, take decisions, simplify complexity and create coherence.

STEADFAST IMPACT

- Having the courage and conviction, under intense and continuous scrutiny, to stay true to yourself and the values of your organization.
- The ability to do so whilst adapting to different stakeholder needs.

2 MOVING FORWARD WITHOUT FALLING BEHIND – THE ATTITUDE THAT MATTERS

QUESTIONS THIS CHAPTER ANSWERS ★
What is the mindset that will ensure you succeed?
What can you do to get it?

We all know that guy (because it's usually a guy). He's the one who tells you "things didn't work like that at my last company, in my last job or with my last team". Even after 12 months in the job, he feels the need to preface every sentence with "obviously I'm still new here" even though even a baby is expected to walk within 12 months.

I bet that guy arouses in you the exact same feeling he arouses in everybody else. It is the feeling that makes you want to say, "why don't you just go back to your last company, job or team?"

You don't want to be that guy!

If we are to succeed in our endeavor to get you that top job, we need to make sure others see you as a credible executive. What we can't afford is for them to think, "why don't you go back to your job" even before you have left it!

Yet, by reading this book and applying the necessary practices you need to get the role you seek, you will also potentially be gaining a few WMA (weapons of mass alienation). Let me explain.

I'm sure you will know someone who, after completing a training programme, returned weirder rather than more skillful. This weirdness stems from two common mistakes people who have just been trained make.

Either they strut around the office with that "this training program just confirmed to me how great I am" attitude everyone hates. Or they become completely obsessed with being/doing that new thing they learned, even if the opportunity for it never actually arises.

There is a tried and tested way to avoid being the annoying or weird one, and instead become the chosen one. That way is adopting the right mindset.

Having the right mindset will protect you. Thinking about mindset before anything else will give you a "non-alienation shield".

The reason your current mindset might not be the right one was summarized by uber-coach Marshall Goldsmith in the title of his bestselling book "what got you here won't get you there".

We climb the organizational pyramid by doing more of what we do. We get promoted because we have more knowledge or more skill. We sell more. We take faster decisions. We make better choices. In short, we personally achieve.

In time, this drive to personally achieve becomes its own reward. When we achieve, we feel good. When we feel good, we do more of the same. When we do more of the same, we grow our achievement mindset further and on and on it goes.

But here is the problem. There comes a point in your career when doing more achieves very little. In fact, there comes a point in your career when personally doing more becomes counter-productive. If you are reading this book, you have reached that stage in your career.

This is why "that guy" always talks about his previous jobs, or that freshly trained manager tells you she knew everything already or tries a newfound tactic at every opportunity even when that opportunity doesn't exist. All they are trying to do is to achieve personally.

Think of a sales person, much beloved of organizational psychologists, so easy are they to understand! The role of a sales person is to sell. The more they sell the more valuable they become, and the more valuable they become the more promoted they are.

Eventually, as the organization runs out of rungs on the ladder or cash on its pay scales, sales people invariably become sales directors and invariably the best sales person becomes the worst sales director.

The reason is simple. The role of a sales director is the exact opposite of that of a sales person. To succeed, a sales person needs to sell; whilst a sales director can only succeed by making other people sell.

Yet, our achievement-driven best sales person knows she can sell better than anyone on her sales force. So, what does she do? She tries to sell on behalf of everyone. She tries to sell twice, three times, ten times as much. Her sales people become demotivated (who wouldn't when the boss is constantly undermining you). The sales director can't sell enough. The numbers fall and so does she.

You see a sales director is not a super sales person. Running faster, working harder, longer or even smarter makes no difference. The sales director role is all about influencing others. It is about coaching, teaching, encouraging. It is not about personally achieving.

What is true of sales people is true of everyone else. Going down the mine at night to dig will never help the CEO of a mining company shift the share price!

Yet, what is simple to understand is not easy to do. The biggest "derailer" on the trajectory to a senior leadership role is the over-arousal of your personal achievement drive. And that's all down to mindset.

So how do you shift your mindset from personal drive to achieve to the need to influence? How do you let go of what has made you successful to date but will more than likely hold you back from now on? How do you embark on this exciting journey to become an executive without risking becoming "that guy"?

Professor of psychology at Stamford University Carol Dweck calls this the "growth mindset" as opposed to the "fixed mindset". You and I may well recognize it as the "experiment and learn" that underpins the scientific mindset.

Whatever you call it, this new mindset is your friend. It will protect you from yourself. Here is how it works.

If you believe that you are already operating at the top of your game[2] and that you have nothing to learn, you are likely to spend your time seeking to prove this. In doing so you will never develop,

....
2. As an aside, it's not a game when so many other people's livelihoods and wellbeing depend on you performing.

thereby entering a kind of self-fulfilling delusion prophecy that leads you nowhere. That's the fixed mindset.

If, on the other hand, you believe that your potential is unlimited and indeed unknown, then you will focus on developing new habits, acquiring new skills and progressing faster. That's the growth mindset.

That's the idea. As counter-intuitive as it might seem, the more focused you are on achieving, the less likely you are to achieve.

So, if you are reading this thinking that the main problem is not that you have something to learn but rather that the world has yet to recognize your greatness, you may want to print a copy of the 5 success mindset habits list at the end of this chapter.

The 5 habits of the success mindset

1. Make a list of what you don't know

Choose one person who has the type of position you aspire to. Make sure they are someone you actually admire/like/think highly of (i.e. someone about whom you don't actually wonder "how on earth did they get that job?"). Write down what it is that they have which you don't by way of skill/knowledge/behavior etc. That list is your proof that there is always something you can learn.

As you continue on your quest, go back to the list once a month and do two things. First put a check mark next to the things you now think you have mastered (there is something therapeutic about putting a check mark against things). Second, enlarge the list by including other people who you don't respect as much, along with the things they do. It may hurt to see them as role models and you may well wonder how they got to where they got to but the truth is, they already have and you haven't yet, which means they still have something to teach you.

2. Set yourself a target you know you can't meet.

There is a good way to establish whether you have the over aroused achievement drive I spoke about earlier. Here are two questions. Do you write to do lists? That's always a good sign but the second one is the acid test. Do you put at the top of that list things that you know you have already almost done or are very easy to do? If you crave achievement, you crave that check mark. If you crave the check mark you will cheat to get it!

The key to having a success mindset is to set challenges you will embrace for no other reason than you will learn something in the process. It doesn't matter if you get the check mark against the output as long as you get the check mark against the process and the effort.

So, make yourself an alternative to do list of things you can't necessarily achieve but the pursuit of which will teach you something. The next part of the book (Boundless Perspective) should offer you plenty of ideas as to what these things might be.

3. Seek feedback on effort and welcome obstacles

It always amazes me how many leaders love to claim accountability for great results (and the associated, mainly financial, benefits they bring), yet shy away from being associated with poor results. The latter are always put down to some external source they had no control over.

The truth is, as always, somewhat greyer.

The one thing we have complete control over is effort. The rest is down to circumstances and we certainly can't control all of these.

The problem with focusing on outcomes over effort is that it leads us to want to avoid circumstances that may lead to different outcomes. Students who are told they have done well (i.e. praised for outcome) as opposed to having worked hard (i.e. praised for effort) are much less likely to engage with progressively more difficult tasks. Why would they when the reward for outcome is less likely when the task gets harder? The reverse is true for students who have been praised for effort.

The same is true for our leadership achievement drive. Seeking feedback on effort helps us focus our energy towards progressively more complex tasks.

With this mindset, obstacles become the fuel to our effort. They become opportunities to learn rather than occasions to fail.

4. Embrace criticisms

Criticism is great. You can learn from it. Don't get me wrong - I do believe in positive feedback. When people tell you what you do well you can integrate this in your routines and do more of it. That's why focusing on your strengths matters. But the success mindset is about focusing on getting better and getting better means seeing criticism as a learning opportunity.

So here is the deal. Make it easy for people to criticize you.

Choose two people whose judgment you trust and ask each one alternatively, once a month (we don't want you to come across as weird and needy) a simple question – "Can you tell me one thing: I could do better/you would have done differently/I shouldn't have done." By the way that's not "three things", just decide on which of the three propositions above you will go with!

When people criticize you, don't go for that old chestnut "it's their problem not mine". You're right, it may well be their problem, but it's a problem they have with you. So, you have to do something about it and the best thing to do is to learn something.

5. Learn from others

Too many leaders, even seasoned ones, feel threatened when meeting other successful people. The success of others should be a source of inspiration not a source of fear. But if you do feel threatened by other people then surround yourself with them!

By surrounding yourself with successful people you won't run the risk of looking like an idiot. In fact, you're much more likely to be looked upon as being one if you always hang around with the other idiots.

So, find the most successful people you can. Make sure they are the ones you feel intimidated by. Go for those who bring out the worst insecurities and behaviors in you. Observe and learn.

Take a blank piece of paper with their names at the top and start recording what they do. Treat it as a piece of scientific research. Look upon them as interesting specimens if you must. But engage and learn. Be inspired by them. Inspiration is the fuel that keeps the success mindset motoring ahead.

I've given you the blueprint and explained the mindset, so now let's start working on doing what executives do.

RECAP

To succeed in adopting leadership habits will require you to adopt a new mindset. Here are the 5 habits that together will reshape the way you think about and approach the challenge ahead.

1. Make a list of what you don't know.
There is always something we don't know and should. If you can't find anything start the list with "humility"!

2. Set yourself a target you know you can't meet.
Having a target will play to your need to achieve. Having a really challenging target will stop you from taking the easy way out.

3. Seek feedback on effort and welcome obstacles.
You may not always be responsible for outcomes, but you will always be responsible for effort. Only feedback on effort can help you get better.

4. Embrace criticisms.
The day people stop criticizing is the day they stop caring. Criticism means someone was expecting something different. Welcome their expectations – the alternative is irrelevance.

5. Learn from others.
Greatness is not something to be feared. Associating yourself with people greater than you does not diminish you. It gives you the opportunity to grow as well as the right people to know.

STEP 1 BOUNDLESS PERSPECTIVE

GETTING BEYOND THE BUSINESS TO LEAD THE BUSINESS

3 STEP-BY-STEP WALKTHROUGH

'Space has always fascinated me. As a young boy looking up at ★ the stars, I found it impossible to resist thinking what was out there and if I ever would experience space first-hand.'
Richard Branson

'The future of humanity is going to bifurcate in two directions: Either it's going to become multi-planetary, or it's going to remain confined to one planet and eventually there's going to be an extinction event.' *Elon Musk*

'All our heavy industry will be moved off planet and earth will be zoned residential and light industrial.' *Jeff Bezos*

What is it with these entrepreneurs and space? Why are they so bothered about it? Is it because they have more money that can be spent here on earth? Is it because they have delusions of grandeur, some kind of God complex that makes them want to conquer the universe? Could it be, more simply, that as they age men just look for bigger toys to play with?

It doesn't really matter what causes their obsession. And whilst the correlation between success in entrepreneurship and interest in space is yet to be demonstrated it is not the topic of this book. What matters for us is the causality between the obsession demonstrated by our three billionaires and their success.

Just as they do in the physical world, boundaries dictate how far your career goes. If you want to make it to the top and thrive once you get there, a boundless perspective is key.

There are a number of reasons why broadening your perspective is a must.

1. The more senior you get, the more complex the levers of value creation become

The more senior you get, the more freedom to act you have. The more freedom to act you have, the more varied your options become. The more varied your options become, the broader the range of relationships you need to unearth possibilities. The creation of value fundamentally changes as roles change.

2. The more senior you get, the broader the range of stakeholders you have.

The voices you must listen to are many and varied. It is no longer good enough to form your views and base your actions on customers' needs and competitors' plays. You not only have to know and respond to the views of analysts, investors, community leaders, regulators etc., but you also have a duty to shape these.

3. A leadership ecosystem is fundamentally different from a managerial one

Success is never singular. To achieve anything in any organization you are always reliant on others. We all perform within a web of relationships. The main difference between an executive role and any other is the nature of that web. Top leaders need networks of value that go well beyond the boundaries of the organization. Whether used to facilitate the flow of information, to connect, collaborate, partner or co-create, this broader and deeper web becomes a strategic asset as opposed to an operational necessity.

The leaders who are masters at this form of perspective all seem to follow a well-established process.

- They somehow manage always to focus on what is relevant.
- They have networks that enable them to keep ahead of environmental changes.
- They know how to translate what they see into value for the organization.

Their success lies in their ability to engineer change rather than be victims of it.

The next three chapters will help you internalize the habits that will ensure you too have this enlarged perspective. They are designed to answer three questions that mirror the process above.

1. With so much going on out there how do I know what is relevant?

How do you spot what will create value amongst the myriad of changes that are going on? How do you differentiate what is interesting from what is critical? The C suite is not an ivory tower. It is not a place of contemplation where you can be Zen-like in your search for meaning. Knowing where to focus is key. Not enough focus and you run the risk of getting lost in data and increasing complexity. Too much focus however will lead to your insights being far too narrow. I urge the executives I work with to develop a 3-circle mindset. In the next chapter I will show you what that entails and share with you some of the techniques you can start using now to unearth value.

2. How do I maintain networks to keep relevant and up-to-date?

There is one thing that is unavoidable when I talk about broadening your perspective and that is having the ability to build strong networks of value. So, the question is what makes networking effective? How can an activity despised by so many be made to work for you? How do you build networks without having to network? The answer is to be found in chapter 5 where I will show you not only how to identify the networks that will add value without wasting your time but also how to engage with them in a way that is fulfilling.

3. How can I translate insights into value?

It is one thing unearthing interesting information and spotting intriguing trends, but it is quite another turning these into value for your organization. The role of the executive is to translate data into information and articulate that information as strategic imperatives others buy into. There is a simple technique that enables you to articulate and disseminate such information in a way that will see you recognized as a credible leader. I call this technique "Shape and Share". We will tackle when to use it and how to master it in chapter 6.

The very idea behind this book begs one last question. How can you add extra value when you don't have extra time?

When first faced with the idea that to become an executive you need to act like one you could be forgiven for thinking that in order to get the job you want, you need to do it on top of the job you have.

Acting like a senior leader doesn't have to mean adding things to your existing role; it just means adjusting your approach to it.

Chapter 7 shows you how you can hack your current job to create your next one. It gives you the lens through which you need to assess your current role to turn your to do list into an opportunity to unleash your leader.

There is one thing our space-obsessed entrepreneurs provide us with and that is an analogy for the perils of rethinking our perspective.

Any institution creates its own gravity. The pull of targets, deadlines, plans and strategies is strong.

Your challenge in embarking on a successful transition is to stay close enough to this gravitational pull so as not to disappear into the ether whilst mastering the spacewalk techniques that will take you to new heights. So, let's boldly go as that famous split infinitive urges us to!

4 THE 3 CIRCLE TECHNIQUE FOR DEVELOPING CURIOSITY WITHOUT DISTRACTION

QUESTIONS THIS CHAPTER WILL ANSWER ★
How do I enlarge my perspective without losing focus?
How do I differentiate what is important from what isn't?

Names like Thomas Young, Joseph Leidy, Athanasius Kircher or Alexander von Humboldt may not be familiar to many people, but they share one thing in common. They were all, in their own time, said to be "the last person to know everything".

In fact, these are not the only names to have received that accolade. Human history is peppered with such people! That is until you get to our most recent history. Whilst we still have intellectual giants and even geniuses, for the last 200 years no one has been awarded that title. We no longer have people who know everything[3].

Given the exponential growth of knowledge this is hardly surprising. Whilst we may like to think of ourselves as knowledgeable, only the deluded would claim to know everything about everything.

But we shouldn't worry. It doesn't really matter.

Today, our problem is not our inability to know everything. Our

---

3. A fact I would rather wasn't disclosed to my children any time soon.

problem is not availability of data. Today, our problem is lack of time.

Our ability to search for information has grown as fast as our ability to generate it. We can always find out what we need to know. But finding out takes time and time is something we haven't got.

And for executives this is a big problem.

Few people assume that executives have a lot of free time. It's true, they don't. From internal meetings to external engagements, the diary of an executive is a nightmare.

However, lack of free time is not the only problem they face. It is their lack of freedom in how they allocate that time that demands a razor-sharp focus.

"I didn't have time to think" is not a valid excuse when a journalist shoves a microphone in your face demanding your view on how a recent breakthrough in nanotechnology will impact your industry as happened to one of our research participants.

So how do you know what to focus on when your time is limited? How do you know what matters to your future when you don't know what this holds?

The answer lies in the three circles framework.

Think of a photo. Any photo. There are always three perspectives in every photo. There is the viewfinder perspective (i.e. the point where the photo is taken). Then there are the foreground and the background.

Now think of yourself as the photographer. When you frame your shot, you think of each of these three perspectives.

The three perspectives

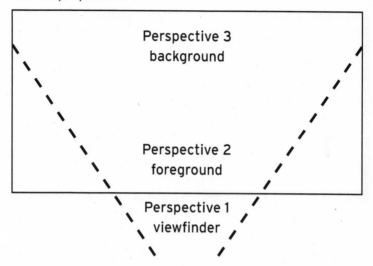

First you must decide where you stand. You need to be steady and you need to be sure your equipment is pointed in the right direction.

Then you assess the foreground. You make sure that there is a tree branch in the way to give the picture depth. You avoid the car parked to your left, as its bonnet would look messy in the shot.

Finally, you look at the background. You want to capture that sky and particularly a weird cloud shaped like a bunny.

Above all you do these three things at once because you want a nice picture (i.e. the viewfinder, foreground and background make one picture not three).

Top leaders apply the same principles when they look at their businesses. However, they use a 360-degree camera.

I call these three perspectives "in, on and out of the business". They are the perspectives that underpin our three circles technique.

The three circles

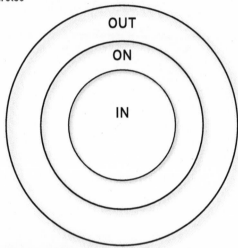

The three circles technique

The demands made on you, as a leader, fall into three circles. What top leaders mean when they identify the need for boundless perspective is the need to keep all three circles in check at all times.

- **The "IN the business" circle**

The IN circle is your viewfinder. It comprises all the demands that are important to delivering results today. They are the important (you have to focus on them) and immediate (they have to be done quickly) tasks. However, being short-term focused they are low leverage.

These are the jobs that you need to do now to meet your objectives. They are necessary for results (e.g. meeting a client, selling something, having a meeting with one of your team members about a new product launch…) but being low leverage, they do not build assets and therefore do not ensure long-term success.

If you only operate "IN the business", you will be successful this year but will be in the same place next year and the one after. More importantly for us you cannot possibly be a successful leader by purely operating in this circle.

- **The "ON the business" circle**

The ON circle is the foreground. It includes the important activities (you know you should focus on them) that do not require immediate attention for short-term success.

However, whilst they do not have to get done now, these are high leverage activities (i.e. there is no negative consequence for not doing these tasks immediately but there are long term benefits).

These activities are things like the shaping and management of talent, the reviews of processes, the planning phase that you know you should do more than once a year.

The activities are potentially transformational but as they have no immediate impact we tend to deprioritize them.

- **The "OUT of the business" circle**

This circle is our background. Unlike the previous two it does not include any of the activities that are related to achieving your business objectives. The OUT circle is all about disruption, be it in the form of opportunities or threats.

Unlike IN the business there is no immediate impact and unlike

ON the business there are no assets to be built. This circle is about creating new possibilities.

There are two ways to tackle this circle. One is to ask the big, bold and radical questions about your business (i.e. why do we even do what we do?). The other is to look at any emerging pattern in science, technology and society and to ask how this could be of any use to what we do.

The key to having a boundless perspective is to know how to have a three-circle perspective.

Remember the photo analogy - no picture is ever perfect if you only focus on getting one of the three aspects right. The executive who had to answer the nanotech question could only credibly do so with a full IN, ON and OUT perspective.

Having boundless perspective is not only about having the curiosity to find out but also having the ability to prioritize different tasks. It is often said that "people speak thin but eat fat" as a way to describe the gap between what we know we should do and what we actually do. The same reality applies to executives. Whilst many "speak strategy" their days are filled with "acting operationally".

So how should you tackle each of the circles in practice?

How to get a 360-degree view

To act like an executive, you must focus on the right issues in each of the circles.

In order not to get lost it is best to understand each circle as containing two questions.

The IN Circle contains two "what" questions. "What" questions are fundamentally about what we need to do and deliver. They are about an immediate perspective. The two driving questions are:

1. **What is the nature of my task?**
2. **What is the nature of my team?**

The ON circle contains two "how" questions. "How" questions force us to think more broadly about what we do. They exist to make us think about our business in a different light. The two driving questions are:

1. **How do I create value for the enterprise?**
2. **How do I increase collaboration in the enterprise?**

Finally, the OUT circle contains two "why" questions. Why questions make us challenge boundaries. They enable us to look beyond our business to discover new opportunities. The two driving questions are:

1. **Why do we do what we do?**
2. **Why do we have a right to exist?**

These questions are your research agenda. They focus you on the right issues and ensure you don't waste the time you haven't got on peripheral (yet, I am sure, fascinating) issues.

Now let's think about how to find the information you need for each of the circles.

Searching in the IN circle

As an executive your job is to create alignment. Alignment is created through clarity and standards. The two "what" questions are designed to check both.

The three questions

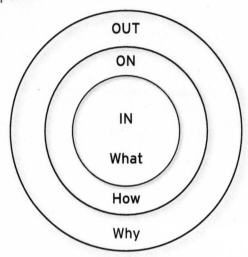

- **What is the nature of your task?**

This question should prompt you to search for clarity. Its answers will enable you to gauge if people know what tasks constitute their role and if they are clear on how those tasks roll up to the big picture.

Your time in the IN circle should be spent on asking people what they are focusing on and ensuring they are clear and aligned.

In your current role this means completing your tasks and ensuring these add up to the mission you have been set. If you have direct reports then you should aim to ensure they do the same.

The information you seek in the IN circle is best found through conversations and observation. Walk around your business. Observe what people do. Talk to them. I know it sounds pedestrian but when was the last time you took time out to do this?

As a senior leader you will have to do this more broadly than just amongst your immediate team. So as an aspiring senior leader you will have to do this more broadly too. If you are in marketing, think about the clarity and standards in sales. Are both departments aligned?

• **What is the nature of my team?**

This question prompts the standards to be set. Here you want to assess the make-up of the talent you have. Do they all work towards the same objective? Have you got capability gaps? Are their targets and compensation setting them on a collision course with each other?

There are plenty of appraisals and assessments in businesses these days. Rather than just use these twice a year (objective setting at the start and compensation allocation at the end) why don't you use them for what they were intended? That alone should set you up to be seen as different!

The main change from your current role to one of top leader is one of scope of research. Executives need to care about the enterprise over the division. Not all of them do but all of them know they should and most of them do a good job of pretending.

So, check the strength of your talent bench at least twice a year. Ask yourself who are the 5 people you can't afford to lose in your division and the 20 in your organization. Get to know them better and get information from them on where the pain points are.

The higher you go in an organization the less likely you are to know the reality of your organization on the ground. Do not assume therefore that the people who matter are the senior people. Get to know at least one highly talented person at every level of your organization.

Think about how effective the connections between the key people are and act as the glue between these connections.

Investigation based on these two questions should already be an integral part of your role but it is now the bedrock of your success as you move towards a top leadership role.

Searching in the ON circle

As well as alignment for the creation of value today, leaders have to think about how value will be created tomorrow.

There are two elements that ensure the continued delivery of value. One is a constant and consistent focus on optimizing organizational processes. The second is ensuring that the organization is seamless in its delivery of value (i.e. that the organizational divisions add up). This is what working ON the business is about.

To narrow your search in this circle there are two questions you need to ask.

• **How do I create value for the enterprise?**

This is the question that will help you surface what can be optimized for improvement. Your IN the business research will have already helped you identify problems so your ON the business search is one for solutions.

This is where you should be looking to your industry peers and competitors for help if you are looking at industry specific challenges (e.g. supply chain), or more broadly for non-industry specific challenges (e.g. developing market insights).

You can get the information you need from your own research or reading, or from your networks. I will get to how you develop a network of value in the next chapter.

The aim here is to think about solutions to how your business works as opposed to solutions to what it does.

The likelihood is that the bulk of the issues you identify will be "stickiness" issues. These are issues where things get stuck in parts of the organization through lack of collaboration (i.e. the proverbial silos). This is where the next question comes in.

• **How do I increase collaboration in the enterprise?**

It may not always be expressed in this way but arguably this is the key question on every leader's mind.

The challenge for any organization is how to reconcile the demands of efficiency with the need for intimacy. As organizations grow (and growth along with return on capital invested is a prerequisite for value), they invariably become fragmented (the need for efficiency drives a need for divisions). The more fragmented the organization becomes the less able it is to adjust quickly to the changing needs of stakeholders.

Ensuring value continues to be delivered lies in our ability to join the dots. This is why collaboration matters.

Searching ON the business means being able to look at the space between the lines on the organization chart. I am not talking about the hackneyed "white space" beloved by innovation consultants. I am talking about the invisible lines of relationships that must be built to make the organization add up.

Think of an organization as two entities – the "formal organization" represented by the organogram and the "real organization" which is the network of relationships between people.

Your job here is to research these relationships. Who could benefit from knowing who? Where are the places where relationships matter? Are these relationships in place? What are people talking about in one part of the business that another part should hear? How do we make information flow as fast as gossip?

These are all questions you can answer through mapping and observation. If relationships are the currency of collaboration, see them in the same way as you see cash. You need to understand how they flow through the business and ensure that flow is uninterrupted.

As I mentioned earlier, my guess is that you would not have reached the level at which you are considering becoming an executive unless you already operated IN and ON the business with some confidence. Whilst the leadership role you aspire to may demand doing some things more widely and broadly than you currently do, the tactics do not fundamentally change.

There is however one circle that, at least in my experience, is less visited by people below senior level. This is our last circle.

Searching in the OUT circle

In her work, strategy and growth guru and Columbia Business School professor, Rita Gunter McGrath, describes the only sustainable competitive advantage as being your ability to learn faster than the rate of change.

Where average leaders see themselves as caretakers of a business, great executives shape it. If you are to be spotted as an executive in waiting, average is not good enough.

Shaping a business requires having the ability to question everything we do in order to get to root causes and breakthroughs whilst at the same time being on the look out for external developments that have the ability to impact, disrupt or indeed improve our business model. A leader must set up the conditions to achieve the level of differentiation necessary for success. The two "why" questions will help you do just that.

- **Why do we do what we do?**

Any proponent of Lean thinking or any other improvement philosophy will tell you that it is only by asking "why" about 5 times that you will get to the root cause of any issue. In the process, you will surface breakthrough and radical thinking of the type that is rare, stands out and is highly valued in any business.

So, whatever the topic to be discussed, problem to be tackled or decision to be made, ask yourself and others "why are we doing this?" Ask the big 'why', not the small one. If you are signing off a request for a new piece of furniture, don't ask "why are we getting it from this supplier?" or "why this piece of furniture?" Instead ask the big "whys" as in "why do we even need furniture?" or "why do we need offices?" The answers to these questions lead to new sources of differentiation.

This is a habit you must have. Remember though "you don't want to be that guy". So maybe until you get comfortable with the technique do it in your head as opposed to out loud. Or maybe practice it with your team before you practice it with your peers or around the board table.

But don't practice for too long. If there is one thing leaders value above anything else from those around them it is truthful radical thinking.

• **Why do we have a right to exist?**

Whilst the first why question focuses on "parts", the second one focuses on "the whole". It is the question that forces you to look at your business model. It is the question that helps you learn and adapt.

Asking why we have the right to exist is not asking for justification. It is asking for an assessment of the fundamental realities that underpin your organization.

Take the example of the insurance industry. Why does it have the right to exist? It does because things go wrong, and people want protection. Now, stop things going wrong, and you remove the right of insurance companies to exist. So, if we introduce a driverless car that has no accidents would it remove the need for car insurance?

I'm not an insurance executive so I don't know whether the answer to that last question is yes or no, but I do know that it is worth asking!

The problem with the OUT circle and the second "why" question in particular is that it tends to be asked only once a year. It tends to remain the domain of yearly strategy offsites and retreats.

At a senior leadership level, this is completely inadequate. The questioning process has to be a continuous assessment of changes and challenges. It has to be a habit.

Practicing it means keeping abreast of any and all changes in our environment. It means a constant focus on scientific and technological developments that lead to societal changes.

You may have heard people say, "leaders are readers". I wish it were true but it's not always the case. Great leaders of sustainable businesses are information magpies though. Whether you get your information through discussing, reading, watching or whatever else you do doesn't really matter.

The key is to get that information and ensure the sources are varied and wide. If you concentrate purely on your industry you will fail. Start with science and tech in general and broaden from there. Set yourself a target to discover 5 interesting things a month and work through what they mean.

This is where you risk getting lost. If you are remotely curious you may end up becoming an academic rather than an executive. This is why you need to make a point of translating the information you get into insights for others – a topic we will turn to in a couple of chapters.

Remember again, the key to the three-circle model is that it is non sequential. You need to work on all three circles at once. Being sequential would be the equivalent of our photographer taking three pictures – one from a great position, one with a beautiful foreground and one with a fantastic background. All of them would be mediocre.

The proportion of time spent in each circle may change but all of them need to be inhabited which takes us back to your time.

How to allocate your time in the right way

Time is a constant. I am not trying to be scientific or philosophical about this - all I mean is that time is a constant topic throughout this book!

There are two reasons for this. One is that top leaders don't have a lot of it so they need to use it carefully[4]. The other is that you now have two jobs to do, your current one and the job of acting as a leader.

So, we need to reflect on how we can allocate your time. In chapter 7 I will show you how you can hack your current job to help you build the attributes you will need for your executive one. In the meantime, though, there is a kind of golden ratio to how much time you should allocate in each circle.

In our research we discovered that most managers split their time in rather predictable ways. The ratio seems to be somewhere between 60 to 70% IN the business 30 to 20% ON the business and 10 to 20% OUT of the business.

This ratio dramatically changes as people progress. The golden ratio for successful executives is, 30/50/20. That's not a hard and fast rule but you should aim to get as close to this split as possible. So here is an idea.

For a month or so, at the end of each week review your diary and decide which of the activities you undertook fitted into which circle. Do this as percentages adding back up to 100 per cent

---

4. I know I have said this a number of times now. You have to believe I am not doing this to waste your time. I am only stressing the point because time is the currency of your need to achieve. You have reached your position because you like doing and people who like doing never seem to have enough time. Consider your lack of time (and the accompanying annoyance with people you feel are wasting it) as the unfortunate consequence of your success!

of your time. And please, don't be one of these talent show acts who promise the judges they'll give "one thousand per cent". It's mathematically erroneous, more than likely unhealthy, probably untrue and downright naff!

After a month, when you have some idea of how you allocate your time, do the time allocation exercise at the start of week. Start the week by deciding how much time you want to spend in each circle aiming to get to the golden ratio. Remember this may not be about doing something different but rather may just necessitate thinking about what you do differently.

Over time, as you build your IN/ON/OUT muscles the whole thing becomes a habit rather than a hindrance. As you change the make-up of your diary you will find that your lack of freedom to allocate your time makes reallocation difficult. This is precisely why we need to find new strategies. The simplest one of these is to outsource some of your thinking.

This is where having networks of value differentiate the best from the rest. Networks help you filter the noise to gain insights quickly. We therefore now need to move on to how to build them and what to do with them.

RECAP

The problem for executives is how to meet the demands of boundless perspective whilst being under time constraints. The answer lies in focusing our search to three circles and six questions.

The IN Circle (the immediate perspective) deals with improving clarity and standards

3. What is the nature of my task?
4. What is the nature of my team?

The ON circle (the foreground) deals with optimizing processes and aligning resources behind them.

3. How do I create value for the enterprise?
4. How do I increase collaboration in the enterprise?

Finally, the OUT circle (the background) provides breakthrough insights.

3. Why do we do what we do?
4. Why do we have a right to exist?

The road to leadership stardom starts with a realignment of our daily routines to ensure the right ratio of perspectives. Whilst most leaders tend to focus primarily IN and ON the business, the most successful amongst them search for a golden ratio of time allocation between the three circles of 30/50/20.

5 YOUR NETWORK IS YOUR NET WORTH – BUILDING NETWORKS WITHOUT NETWORKING

QUESTIONS THIS CHAPTER WILL ANSWER ★

How do I know which networks to choose?

How do I make them work for me?

I hate networking. In fact, I hate networking even more than I hate writing as tired a sentence as "I hate networking". But whilst I hate networking, along with 2.5 billion[5] people, I love networks.

Why is it that we love connections so much that we crave the presence of loved ones, of families, of past friends and colleagues and yet, hate them so much when we have to mingle with acquaintances and strangers at a networking event.

For those of you who, like me, belong to the "let's pretend I'm making a call so no-one talks to me" brigade, the answer is deceptively simple and can unlock the value we get from the networks we ought to belong to.

But first, you might have a much more prescient question.

Why should I bother with networking at all?

My hope is that if I can prove the link between relationships and

5. This is the estimated number of worldwide social media users in 2018.

results and show you how to ensure networking helps you build powerful relationships, I can help you move from "why should I bother?" to "when can I start?"

Think of relationships as the foundation for the pyramid of results. Relationships deliver results. More relationships deliver more results. Better relationships mean better results.

The results to relationships pyramid

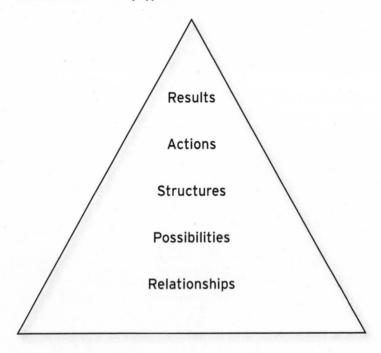

Results

Actions

Structures

Possibilities

Relationships

If we ask ourselves where results come from, the only possible answer is actions. Any sales person staring at her target the whole day will find it hard to achieve anything. Actions beget results.

Through the structures we have put in place, be they processes, business models, tactics, our organizational culture etc., we dictate the nature of the actions we take. If you have a process for example that dictates 10 cold calls a day for one sale to be made, the likelihood is that 10 calls will be made.

It is worth knowing that most leaders focus on the interplay between results, actions and structures alone.

If results are poor, they mandate more actions. Make 20 calls instead of 10. If this makes no difference, then let's increase the target again. Eventually, when the target becomes unachievable or the leader becomes worried, she will call a strategy consultancy for new options (i.e. new structures for fulfillment).

McKinsey or whomever else will oblige and off we go again for another round of actions and results.

The job of the consultant in this instance is simply to unearth the best possible structures for fulfillment out of a range of possibilities. These possibilities could be new technologies available, new best practices being spotted in an adjacent industry, and so on.

The important question for us here is where do these possibilities come from? All possibilities are rooted in relationships. It is relationships that open possibilities which in turn shape structures to dictate the actions that drive our results.

That's why networking matters. It is the vehicle that enables us to build the relationships we need to unearth the possibilities that will increase results.

Networking is not self-promotion. It is not about building a catalogue of contacts that might come in handy. Networking is simply one of the processes that helps us build the relationships we need to enhance our results.

The key to increasing value for your organization and therefore increasing your value as an executive lies in your ability to choose the right networks.

How do I know which network to choose?

Simply put, the right network is the one that will give you maximum value (i.e. new possibilities) for minimum time invested.

There is no such thing as the one perfect network that will deliver everything you need to master boundless perspective. However, here again, our 3-circle technique will help you choose where to invest your time and energy.

The three networks

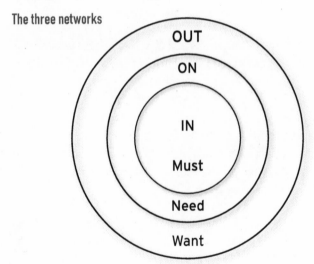

Remember that what we are trying to do is to build networks that will offer us the relationships we need to enhance our perspective (i.e. create new possibilities) IN, ON and OUT of the business.

To maximize return on your time invested it is best to focus on each of the 3 circle dimensions. Ideally, we need one network per dimension (you could aim for more and probably will want to once we get rid of your dislike for, or discomfort with, networking).

Here is how to find them.

Each one of our circles demands a different focus and therefore a slightly different network. As a result, the way to choose them will differ. As shown on the picture above, the best way to think of them is as MUST, NEED and WANT networks.

- **The MUST network**

These are the networks that help you win IN the business.

The reason they are MUST networks is because if you are to maximise your effectiveness you must belong to them. These networks are your professional networks (e.g. professional associations, peer forums etc.).

To be credible as a leader you must be a master of the IN circle. To be a master of the IN circle you must know your stuff and, as importantly, must be seen to know your stuff. To be seen to know your stuff you have to be an influencer in your field, hence the need to belong to a professional network.

The golden ratio tells us you must spend 30% of your time IN the business so don't go overboard on choosing too many MUST networks.

Identify the most important/relevant/high profile one for your profession and sign up. Try to attend at least one event every two to three months. The idea is to get to know what is going on in your profession, identify the latest trends and get tips on how to increase your own and your team's effectiveness.

We will get back to how you translate the information you gain into value for your business in the next chapter. For the time being, your job is to identify the most valuable networks and secure a place on these.

- **The NEED network**

These networks help you set your ON the business agenda.

They are the ones you need to belong to if you are going to optimize your business. They should help you identify new practices and possibilities that can become the best-fit practices in your business.

Given the golden ratio tells us you should spend 50% of your time ON the business, identifying the best NEED networks you should belong to is critical.

This is where consultants are your friends.

NEED networks are industry networks. They unearth what is going on in your competitors' and adjacent industries' businesses. Consulting firms (whether the big strategy houses or consulting arms of accountancy firms) are great at doing this and stage regular events where they share their findings. With a bit of luck your business already works with some of them, so you will be able to avoid the selling side of these events. The added advantage is that most top leaders have relationships with these consultancies and so you should too.

The other option is to identify the business schools that stage networking events. There are a lot of them and in my experience they always welcome leaders who can contribute to their research.

Make sure you belong to a couple of these networks, as they can make a big difference to your business, your credibility and therefore your career.

- **The WANT network**

These networks will help you shape your OUT of the business agenda.

Their focus is on understanding disruptive as well as opportunity-generating forces.

Remember our space-obsessed entrepreneurs? Their focus is on a very specific type of information when they think OUT of the business. These are the STEM topics. STEM (i.e. Science, Technology, Engineering and Mathematics) is where magic happens. They are the areas that are most likely to engender disruption and innovation.

Forget maths for our purpose, as it is after all the underpinning to most of the other topics and replace it with media (as in design, print, social, entertainment etc.) as this is another area of disruption.

Now the reason these networks are called WANT networks is because you get a chance to choose where you go with this. There is no hard and fast rule other than going for something you believe you will enjoy finding out about.

One way to do this is to go back to your childhood. What did you want to be when you grew up? I know from experience that most of us did not want to be what we turned out to do. This is your chance to turn back the clock.

If you wanted to be a vet, why not think about a scientific/medical network? If you wanted to be an artist, then choose an art-based media network? A fire fighter, no worries, go for something to do with engineering…

The point here is to choose a couple of areas of STEMedia you think you will enjoy and decide which networks might engage you the most (you can't choose on the basis of value as you have no idea what value they are likely to deliver).

Think about charitable associations. Make space in your diary to volunteer on the board of a not-for-profit. Contact a university to see if you can teach business to engineers. Think broadly and act quickly. 20% of your networking time needs to be invested on the OUT.

There are plenty of networks to which you can and should belong. Identifying them is not that hard. Following the golden ratio in allocating your time to them should be pretty straightforward. The hardest part however is still to make them work for you.

How do I make networks work for me?

There is a reason I started this chapter by making a distinction between our dislike of networking and love of networks. Social networks, especially offline ones, have always been about relationships. We are social animals. We like them because they help us forge bonds with others.

By contrast, networking tends to be about self-orientation. Whether it is about gaining some new information or displaying personal characteristics, networkers tend to see others as a source of value rather than relationships.

To understand the mindset that will help you make the most of networking you need to understand and master the 5 elements of effective relationship building.

• UTILITY

Relationships start when one person sees value in getting to know another. That is utility. It is useful for you to have relationships with others.

Given this is the foundation of relationships it's easy to understand why so many people spend so much time obsessing about it. The problem is that it is also the root of the self-orientation we all despise.

So yes, you must be clear about the value your networks are supposed to bring. You must be thoughtful about the value people you associate with bring. You must be ruthless in abandoning a network and indeed the people within this if they don't deliver value to you because you must be ruthless with your time.

Networks are friends, not families. You get to choose them. However, to release their full value and build real relationships they must also choose you.

• RECIPROCITY

Reciprocity is when both parties to a relationship find value in it. Networking stalkers please note, without reciprocity there is no relationship!

Reciprocity saves you from self-obsession.

I know you know how to pay attention to others and engage

them. Being someone who others want to work with was one of my "non-negotiables" for progression. That being said, when attending networking events we tend to forget this.

Treat them as treasure hunts. Your task is to search for insights to share with others. To accomplish this, you will need to know more about those attending and in particular their areas of interest. Try to find areas of common interest to discuss with them. More importantly follow up after the event with an added value message targeted to that area. If they like French food and so do you, recommend one of your favorite restaurants in a part of town you know they might not normally go to. If they are fascinated by psychology, tell them about the latest article you read which you found fascinating. Whatever it is, add value.

• SAFETY

Relationships flourish only when they are psychologically safe. Psychological safety is the idea that being yourself will not have negative consequences on your psychological well being. In other words, you won't be made to feel stupid, lesser, weak etc.

The problem with most networking events is they tend not to be psychologically safe. Who would want to ask a question in front of a group of peers? Who is likely to admit to a flaw in front of potential competitors?

Yet for relationships to be of value we need psychological safety. Your job is to start the trend. Ask questions, voice your concerns and disclose your fears so others can do the same.

You don't want to force it as otherwise you'll only end up making up questions which are likely to be ones nobody else would ever ask. But not forcing it isn't the same as not starting it.

- **WARMTH**

No one wants to associate with dour people for too long. I know networking has the word 'work' in it, but it doesn't mean that you have to forget your humanity.

Make it fun for others to be with you. Tell stories and disclose something about yourself. You don't have to make friends for life, but you do have to be more than an insight-seeking machine.

Think as a human doing (what will be useful for my work) and wanting (what do I want to get out of this) but engage as a human being!

People are more likely to trust you and share with you if they feel they know you.

- **MAINTENANCE**

Maintenance is all about being accessible. Relationships start going wrong when people feel they can't get close to you or get hold of you. That's when it stops being fun, becomes less safe as a consequence and makes people question the reciprocal nature of the relationship and, as a result, its utility.

There are two moments that define maintenance. The first is during meetings/events and the second is afterwards.

During an event be fully present. Ditch the phone and email and stay the course. If you find you need distraction, then the network is not the one you should belong to.

After the event, follow up and continue to engage. Send the emails I talked about earlier and continue conversations. You may gain more insights others weren't prepared to share at the meeting. So be present in the moment and keep in touch after the event.

Networking is not going away. It is still, to this day, the best way for a leader to get the information necessary to develop the boundless perspective she needs to succeed.

Opportunities to network are everywhere. All you have to do is to change your mindset from one of information-seeker to relationship-builder.

Networks will offer you all the data you need. What we now need to think about is how to turn the data you gather into the value that will differentiate you.

RECAP

To get more and better results you need more and better relationships. Relationships open up new possibilities and new possibilities unlock new actions. This is why networking matters.

How to choose the networks you need

To ensure that you gain value without wasting time there are three types of networks you need to belong to.

- THE MUST NETWORKS
  These are the networks that help you win IN the business. They are profession specific and help you discover best practices for the work you do.

- THE NEED NETWORKS
  These networks help you set your ON the business agenda. They are industry specific and focus on adjacent practices.

- **THE WANT NETWORKS**
  The focus of these networks is on understanding disruptive as well as opportunity generating forces. They will help you shape your OUT of the business agenda.

How to make them work

Ensuring that networking becomes value generating (if not a joy) is about applying the 5 elements of relationships effectively.

- **UTILITY**
  Be clear on the value your networks are supposed to bring and be ruthless in abandoning them if they don't deliver.

- **RECIPROCITY**
  Search for insights to share and areas of common interest to discuss with others in your network.

- **SAFETY**
  Ask questions, voice your concerns and disclose your fears so others do the same.

- **WARMTH**
  Think as a human doing and wanting, but engage as a human being

- **MAINTENANCE**
  Be present in the moment and keep in touch after the event.

6 SHAPE AND SHARE – HOW TO BRING VALUE THAT STANDS OUT

QUESTIONS THIS CHAPTER WILL ANSWER ★

How do I transform the information I gained into value for the organization?

How do I share this for maximum impact?

Aimlessness is to leaders what a vacuum is to nature - they abhor it.

Yet, in our search for boundless perspective we haven't spent much time discussing the goal of the search. But there is a reason why I gave you targeted specific questions rather than targeted specific criteria for your IN/ON/OUT inquiries and your MUST/NEED/WANT networking.

Possibilities are born out of serendipity and obliqueness. When we search for something targeted and specific we ignore what is adjacent. We reduce rather than enlarge our perspective. We miss interesting, related yet not immediately connected, facts. It is therefore important to read, question and network with an open mind.

However there comes a point when we need to create value. We need to construct insights and share these in a way that makes others act on them. That's the "why" of boundless perspective.

These two acts of SHAPING the information you have into valuable insights and SHARING them for action encapsulate the last discipline of boundless perspective.

Let's unlock each in turn.

How do I transform the information I gained into value for the organization?

The idea here is to merge the information you gained from your IN/ON/OUT focus with the data you gathered from your MUST/NEED/WANT networks. This exercise is about organizing information in a way that will help you unearth value quickly.

One of the executives we interviewed during our research uses a simple framework we call the 3 Ps for Problems, Pain points and Possibilities[6].

The 3 Ps of value making

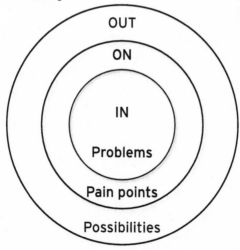

---

6. I know technically that should be 4 Ps given Pain and Points each start with P but that would be confusing as there are only three categories!

- **IN the business PROBLEMS**

Problems are immediate and time bound (e.g. We did not close a sale. We missed a deadline. We sent out faulty products). They sit IN the business and need to be remedied quickly.

In chapter 4 when I introduced the IN the business circle I asked you to focus on two "what" questions:

1. **What is the nature of my task?**
2. **What is the nature of my team?**

Asking these questions should have surfaced a number of problems that need to be remedied. The solutions to these problems will lie in two places.

The first place is the people who told you about the problems. Chances are that the very reason they outlined a problem was to share with you their view of how it could be solved. Of course, in the vast majority of cases, their answer to the problem will be to point out how ineffectual or inefficient someone else is (we seldom see problems in the way we operate personally)! That does not mean you should dismiss their views. If they identify someone else as the source of the problem, go and talk to them too and see things from their perspective. This will enlarge the circle of possibilities.

The second place you can go to for answers to problems is the knowledge you gained from your MUST networks. Can you find practices that have been used by others facing similar problems? Is there a way you could discuss some of your issues with the contacts you have made?

By tapping into the collective knowledge of the people inside your organization and the wisdom of those outside it you will find solutions to your IN the business problems.

If a problem is a recurring one, then it becomes a pain point and should be treated as such.

- **ON the business PAIN POINTS**

Unlike problems, pain points are not immediate issues. They are themes that underscore sub-optimized structures and processes. They lie in the "how" of the business, which is why, if you recall, we looked at two questions when searching ON the business.

1. **How do I create value for the enterprise?**
2. **How do I increase collaboration in the enterprise?**

Like problems, pain points depend on a backward look at your business. We need to identify things that have happened. To do this, look back at the relationships you studied when working ON the business.

Identify the areas where relationships are few and far between. This could indicate an opportunity. Look for hubs (i.e. areas where many relationships start and end). These could be bottlenecks.

You should also try to identify themes coming out of your own reading and research as well as your NEED networks. What are others talking about? What pain points are talked about the most and what solutions are offered?

Ask yourself these four questions when addressing pain points. What happened? Why did it happen? What conclusions can I draw from this? What can I do with them? These will force you to observe, reflect, conclude and act in a logical way. Miss any of the steps and your recommendations are likely to be misguided.

Just like with driving however, looking back doesn't take you very far (at least not safely). To really increase value and make a noticeable difference (and, more importantly given our purpose, one that is noted by others), you need to add forward value. This is the domain of possibilities.

- **OUT of the business POSSIBILITIES**

I started this chapter by stating that leaders abhor aimlessness. Yet, countless research papers show how it and its cousin, boredom, enhance creativity. That's why you have your best thoughts in the shower! Here is how it works.

Think of the brain as a puddle. Now think of your IN/ON/OUT investigations and your MUST/NEED/WANT networking as jumping in the puddle. As you may recall from your childhood, when you jump in a puddle the water goes murky. The sediment gets all mixed up. If you leave the water alone however everything settles down and the water becomes clear again. Boredom is your brain's way of making your thoughts become clear again.

When I proposed the two "why" questions of OUT of the business thinking (Why do we do what we do? Why do we have a right to exist?) I was asking you to jump in the puddle. The way to get clarity is to let these thoughts stew and STEW is the acronym we will use to make sure you can do this with some focus and speed (because I know that asking you to get bored is not the best strategy to ensure you turn the page).

To gain value from your OUT of the business activities, organize your findings under these four STEW categories.

1. SURPRISES

Whenever you come across something you've never heard of, thought of or simply never cared about, that something will have value. Surprises are always an indication of some newly acquired knowledge.

Turning that newfound knowledge into value starts with asking yourself the question "Why was this a surprise?" Is it because no-one in my business is talking about it? Is it because they are but I haven't been keeping up? Should they? Should I have?

2. THEMES

From "crypto currencies" to "customer experience", from "agile" to "digital" via "blockchain," there are themes that seem to hit most disciplines as well as businesses. What are the ones you've identified? What could they mean for your organization? Is your business doing anything about them already?

3. EXTREMES

In business we are trained to ignore extremes. That's why we always do three business cases, and all agree on the middle one. But extremes provide the most value when it comes to boundless perspective precisely because they are most often discounted.

The best way to find extremes is to look for the data points you automatically put in the box labeled "But we're not like this" or "It couldn't work for us". From businesses that set no targets for their employees to those that have dispensed with managers altogether, there are plenty of examples of extremes that will make you question the "whys" of your business.

4. WEIRD STUFF

Finally, if you have come across anything else you found strange yet interesting which does not fit into any of the three categories above put it down here. As a rule, today's weird stuff becomes tomorrow's trend so you're not wasting your time.

The trick is not to forget about this list. Go back to it regularly and see if your puddle has settled down and clarity has come to the surface.

The 3 Ps work under the same rule as the golden 30/50/20 ratio so make sure that your insights align with it (30% answers to problems, 50% solutions to pain points and 20% possibilities). This exercise is not a one off. It is an ongoing endeavor. Don't feel that you need to share all your insights at once. Choose your battles on the basis of the amount of potential value they will add.

Having answers to problems, enduring solutions to pain points and innovative possibilities is only of value if something is done about them. This means we now need to think about how you share your insights in a way that makes others want to act on them.

How do I share my insights for maximum impact?

Vying for a place in the pantheon of overused and flawed business sentences alongside "what gets measured gets done" is "let the facts/data speak for themselves".

The facts never speak. The data, to paraphrase British economist Ronald Coase, if tortured for long enough, will confess to anything. And us humans, regardless of what is said, will seldom really listen.

But there is one way to ensure people listen. There is one way to guarantee engagement. That way is stories. Now I know what you're thinking. Leaders aren't children, how can they be engaged by stories?

Here are three reasons you ought to change your mind.

For a start, leaders may not be children, but they have roughly the same attention span as any three-year-old.

Second every leader has one blind spot (due to their position rather than their intent). They have no idea what actually, really, goes on, on a day-to-day basis, inside their business. They know this, so they crave these stories.

Finally, the very definition of stories is "narratives designed to interest" which is exactly what we're after.

You would be a weird adult if you ever thought it appropriate to tell a story to a child with bullet points and slides. Sharing insights with a view to generating action means finding the right story to tell and telling it in the right way.

There are 5 elements to the way we craft and tell stories that make others want to hear them and act on them. The "5 Cs of sharing for action" are your style guide to sharing your insights.

• **COMPELLING**

Engaging people with facts and data, or indeed any information, requires just that - engagement. For engagement to happen there has to be a prize. The facts will only speak if someone is willing to listen and they will only listen when they are interested.

Whether it is interest in solving an issue, interest in the outcome or just interest in the story, interest is a pre-requisite to action.

The only way to make your story compelling is to link what you have to say to a prize you know your audience will care about. That means knowing your audience and their preoccupations. Value is in the eye of the audience not the storyteller.

- **CONCISE**

An HR Director client of mine uses the phrase "give me the baby but spare me the labor pains" as a way to express displeasure with longwinded preambles. You might not like the analogy, but you had better get used to the sentiment.

Remember, leaders are busy so get to the point. If you don't, they will assume you don't have one.

Being concise will depend on your ability to be clear. Enough said!

- **CLEAR**

You know you have failed in convincing someone to act on the basis of your recommendations when you hear either of these two questions "so what's the point?" or "so what?"

Be clear on what the prize is. Be clear on what you want and what you need.

Training yourself to express your point in one sentence can seem reductive but it is a great way to ensure it is clear.

The clearer you are about your point the shorter the amount of time you will require to express it.

When entrepreneurs pitch to Venture Capitalists they use a "pitch deck" that contains only 10 slides. These are Purpose, Problem,

Solution, Why now, Market/Opportunity size, Product/Solution, Team, Business Model, Competition and Financials.

Use a combination of these to frame your story (but don't use the slides to share it). It will help you achieve the clarity you seek.

- **CREDIBLE**

If your story was ever turned into a book it should sit in the non-fiction category. Too many people still think of stories as fiction or at least dramatic exaggeration.

Sure, an element of drama will keep people intrigued and engaged but the story needs to be credible. To be credible it needs to be expressed in a way that resonates with the audience.

In practice, what this means is that your story needs to be rooted in facts and illustrated with real examples. It should be shared with eloquence, but it must be backed up by evidence.

It is not just your story that needs to be credible; you too need credibility. That means choosing the way you share your story carefully. I hope my experience and expertise gives me the credibility I need to share the story of leadership transition with you. I do know however that I would have little credibility writing a book on "Pricing American-type Parisian Options"[7].

Of course, the aim of this book is to get you out of your sphere of expertise, so you can influence things outside this. To do so successfully, make sure you have the back up of credible allies and that you do your homework.

....

7. I have no idea what this means but it came up when I googled "most complex investment products"!

- **CONSISTENT**

Finally, to engage others, you and your story will need to be consistent with the purpose of your business.

It is fine to make a case for a change of direction or strategy. However, remember that if you want to argue that you are in the wrong business you will need to do a lot more than tell a story. If you don't you may find the leaders you are trying to engage conclude that it is you who are in the wrong business.

Consistency is also about sticking to your message until proven wrong (and you should be prepared to be proven wrong), as well as ensuring that the messages you share are consistent with each other. In a thirst for making points, or trying to impress or please, too many aspiring executives will argue one thing one day and another the next.

Again, this comes back to choosing your battles carefully.

The biggest risk with Shape and Share is that you unearth so much value along the way that you become driven to being part of every conversation about every topic.

Remember that the audiences you choose will differ depending on the issues you tackle. Not everything needs to be fedback "upwards". The majority of your IN the business insights will be shared with your team whilst most ON the business pain points can be dealt with alongside your peers.

If this all feels like a lot of work over and above your "day job" it's because it is. So, to have a chance to achieve any of this we need to find a way to make as much of it as possible fit into your existing schedule.

Luckily there is a way to hack your day job to achieve your dream one and that's what I want to share with you next before we move on to the second unique characteristic of top leadership roles.

RECAP

Adding value is the surest way to be spotted as an executive in waiting. To do so requires you to SHAPE the information you gained from your research and networks into valuable insights and know how to SHARE these for impact.

How to shape information into insights.

Organize your findings into these three categories.

- IN the business PROBLEMS
  Match the problems you unearthed when working IN the business with the solutions you gained from your MUST networks.

- ON the business PAIN POINTS
  Use your ON the business investigations to spot recurring issues that can be solved using insights from your WANT networks.

- OUT of the business OPPORTUNITIES
  Complexity is increasing at roughly the same rate as are demands on our time. The more we focus on what we have to do, the more we miss the opportunities offered by what we could be doing. By mixing your OUT of the business interests with your WANT networks' insights you can sift through the myriad of possibilities others don't see to bring them the value they seek.

How to share your insights for impact:

- CONCISE
  Leaders are busy so get to the point. If you don't, they will assume you don't have one.

- CLEAR
  Summarize your point in one sentence. It's not reductive, it's clear.

- CREDIBLE
  Your point is like a document on your computer. If you don't back it up, it risks being lost.

- COMPELLING
  If you can't make your proposal relevant, you can't make it exciting. If you can't make your proposal exciting, don't make your proposal.

- CONSISTENT
  You can either be consistent (with the purpose of your business and the positions you take) or you can be ignored. Your choice!

7 HACKING YOUR DAY JOB TO GET YOUR DREAM JOB

QUESTIONS THIS CHAPTER WILL ANSWER ★
How can I add new practices to my job when I have so much on already?
How do I focus on the next role when there are so many distractions in my current one?

I knew nothing about the two men in front of me at the check-in counter apart from the fact that they worked for an organization that still allowed its employees to fly business class on short haul flights. By the time we got to board the flight, however, I could have told them how their careers would unfold.

Don't get me wrong, I don't profess to see the future, nor do I subscribe to the idea that you can diagnose psychological traits and relational outcomes through overheard conversations.

My level of certainty simply came down to two things: odds, plus our relationship with time. The odds of either of them being successful moving forward were low and I knew this because of their flawed relationship with time.

These two men were engaged in a game of "busyness" poker.

When one said he would have to get straight to the hotel as soon as the flight landed at 22:00 to have a call with his boss, the other laughed that he couldn't check in until 2 a.m. because he had to go straight to a dinner with potential clients.

When one stated he was too busy to go to his son's football game, the other replied that he'd only found out that weekend that his son had started playing football a year earlier.

The conversation continued and touched on bonuses, promotions and sales targets but always in the same way. Both men were trying to outbid each other in a weird auction where the key prizes were "who gets the least sleep" and "who knows least about their children".

It may well have been one of the saddest conversations I have ever overheard but it was also just an extreme example of the conversations most people have in most businesses on most days.

We have come to measure our value in inverse proportion to the time we have. This is not only sad - it is destructive.

Increasing your activity will not increase your chances of promotion. Spending more time at work will not give you better results. In fact, the opposite will happen.

Increasing your activity will decrease your ability to see the wood from the trees. Spending more time IN the business will decrease your opportunity to spend more time ON or OUT of it.

Sure, working hard is necessary to succeed. Sure, some will need to work harder and not simply smarter. But if you have read past chapter one I have to believe that you meet the basic conditions I set out for success. And if you meet the basic conditions, then my guess is that you are already working at full capacity.

You don't have any spare time.

To increase your odds of success, we need to hack your relationship with time at work, not simply spend more time at work.

Whilst you may have to add some new routines to your existing schedule, we need to make sure that you don't fall into the trap of thinking that more activity equates to a greater chance of getting promoted.

There are two things we need to work out – how do we make time and how do we make the most of your time.

Firstly, we'll need to work out if we can release some of your time so we can add new practices into your daily routine.

If we can't release enough time (which is likely) then we'll need to work out how to incorporate new activities into your existing ones.

We'll need to ensure that we maximize the return on your time invested. Whatever you do must bring you success in your current role as well as take you closer to your new one.

Our aim should be to ensure that you keep your eyes on the goal without taking them off your role.

How can I add new practices to my job when I have so much on already?

No offence intended but as a successful person you are somewhat predictable. When something needs to be done, you do it. When more needs to be done, you work harder.

That's a good thing. It has made you successful. It is also however no longer sustainable.

There is not enough time during the day for you to take on the job of an executive on top of the job you currently hold. So how do we make time in your busy schedule for some of the new activities I have advocated in the last few chapters?

We need to delegate some of your tasks. Bear with me here. I know you're probably rolling your eyes at the idea of delegation. You're probably thinking that delegation is something first line managers talk about on training courses. You're right. They do.

There is however a surprising finding coming out of the research we conducted for this book. You may recall that I mentioned earlier that not only do leaders not have enough time, but also that they don't have control over their time. The fact is that your diary gets filled by other people with things that you take for granted you have to do. However, when we worked with executives' diaries we, and they, discovered that some of the activities that had crept into their schedules could indeed be easily delegated.

So first make a list of what you got up to over the last four weeks. Four weeks is important. It will allow you to see your full range of activities.

Split them into the IN, ON and OUT categories we talked about earlier. Having done so, focus on the IN activities. Could any of these activities be delegated?

Legitimately there will be some activities that only you can conduct. However, before you decide that all activities fall into this category, there are a couple of things to think about.

The first is the eternal issue of you being the best at what you do. Whether you are in finance, sales, marketing, production, procurement or whatever else you are into, the reason you have reached your position is that you are the best at what you do. Great. Good for you. You are the best finance, marketing, sales or whatever person. Congratulations!

But if this is what you identify yourself as, and you take pride in it, then why on earth would you want to be anything different? I know you are better than other people at what you do. Our task however is to turn you into the best senior leader.

If you identify yourself as the best marketer, why would you expect others around you to see you as anything other than that?

Unless you are prepared to shift your self-image, you will be reluctant to delegate either because you don't think anyone will do things as well as you or because you enjoy doing them too much to let them go. Both will stand in the way of your progress.

The second reason you might be quick to allocate tasks to the "I have to do these myself" category is that you don't trust others to do them properly.

The truth is that if your people aren't good enough to take on the jobs you are looking to delegate, then your job is to make sure they are and to do this as quickly as possible.

This is slightly different from the above. It is not about whether you are any good at delegating. Instead, it is about whether they are any good at delivering.

Let's be clear about trust here. I am not talking about whether you would trust these people to look after your kids or elderly relatives.

I am not asking you to trust them with whatever your pride and joy is. Let's not pretend this is some kind of deep and meaningful insight about the depth of your relationship with them. I am simply asking whether you trust them to deliver.

Do you believe that they can successfully achieve the challenges you set for them? We have established that they are unlikely to be as good as you, but will they be any good at all?

You need to focus on the drivers of trust. Are they credible (i.e. do they know their stuff)? Are they reliable (i.e. do they do what they say)? Do they have your or their best interests at heart? By asking yourself these three questions you can start to define some of the root causes of your potential discomfort and address them. If you do that then you will be able to define the type and amount of delegation possible.

So having decided what you can delegate to whom, you should now be left with the activities that, indeed, only you are legitimately capable of undertaking.

Hopefully, in the process, we have managed to release some of your time. On the basis that we are trying to get you closer to the 30/50/20 ratio and that we will be able to get you to work ON the business more with our next step you should allocate this new-found time to OUT of the business activities.

Now we have exhausted all possibilities to make more time we need to focus on how we make the most of your time.

How do I focus on the next role when there are so many distractions in my current one?

Not having enough time is not as big a problem as it first appears.

Think back to my fellow conscript Pitiot. There was no way he could do the job of an officer on top of doing his job of trainee soldier!

Indeed, Pitiot didn't have the time. Our Sergeant would have made sure of that. But that was not his only issue.

Even if he had managed to find the time, he would have annoyed everyone around him. Officers wouldn't have liked someone acting above his station and fellow conscripts would have hated someone dropping the ball on soldier duties. And in any case, he would have required more stamina than any human being could have displayed.

So, what could he have done?

The answer is simple yet hard to put into practice. He could have done his current role but done this in the way an officer would have approached it.

This is what you need to attempt to remedy the fact that you have to include new practices in an already busy schedule. The existing tasks you have to conduct can provide you the opportunity to get your next role. The trick is to do them differently.

Having reviewed your tasks, your diary should now be filled with mainly IN the business components, followed by some, albeit limited, ON the business ones and a few OUT of the business activities we've managed to add in by freeing some of your time.

Our task is to think how we can use your remaining IN the business tasks to gain ON the business insights.

Let's imagine for a moment that you are in marketing and one of your tasks is to review the agencies on your preferred supplier list[8]. The IN the business way of doing this is to just get on with it and review the list.

Rather than just completing the task, the executive approach is to try to derive lessons from it. In the case of our marketer, she may want to ask a number of how (ON the business) questions and why (OUT of the business) questions rather than just focusing on the what.

How did we end up with so many agencies in the first place? Why do we use agencies at all? How are other parts of the business coping with their suppliers? How can I share my methodology more broadly with them, or indeed understand the methodology they may be using? Could we not rethink the way we do marketing on the back of this?

You see where I am going with this. The point is that doing something, anything, has implications and these implications are the things senior people care about.

If you want to be seen as a leader you have to go beyond the what. You can't ignore the what. You have to be the best at the what. But you can't just do the what.

The answers to the "how" and "why" questions are the valuable findings you can share. The key is for you to approach every task as an opportunity to learn something you can then share.

Making the most of your time means surfacing lessons for your team, your peers and your superiors. This means you need to understand what they will see of value as well as decide on the

---

8. I guess marketing people do this every now and again. I'm not sure if senior people like you get involved in this kind of thing but humor me for the sake of the example. The point will still be valid irrespective of which activity you want to consider.

most effective way to teach it (remember you don't want to be "that guy").

Success will not be about working harder or indeed smarter; instead it is about working wider. To have a boundless perspective will require you to see every bounded task as an opportunity to surface a boundless lesson!

You can work IN/ON/OUT of the business during one conversation. Imagine for example that you have been asked to meet with your team to discuss the allocation of end of year bonuses. Deciding on who gets what is an IN the business task. You could however easily take an ON the business perspective by asking if the bonus allocation system is in line with the values of the organization. Indeed you may even take things a step further and ask "why do we pay people anyway?" which could take you OUT of the business towards a discussion around motivation and effort.

You may never get to the magic ratio of 30/50/20 but by being more diligent about your time allocation and your return on time invested, you can get a lot closer to it than you may first have thought possible.

RECAP

To succeed, you will need to integrate the practices described in previous chapters into your daily routine. This means that you will either have to make more time or make more of the time you have.

How can I start practicing the new habits when I can't give up the old ones?

To help you answer this question we need to think about how you make more time in your schedule. Assess your daily activities carefully and decide whether you genuinely and legitimately have to undertake them all yourself.

There will always be some you can delegate. Decide if you trust the people you have around you to perform these tasks. Think about their intent, capability and track record. This will tell you how much effort you need to invest in developing them prior to being able to develop yourself.

This should save you some time that you can allocate to some of the OUT of the business activities you identified in earlier chapters.

How can I focus on the new role when there are so many distractions in my current one?

When you have decided on the tasks that you should legitimately focus on personally, the trick is to think about how to approach them with a leadership mindset.

This means that whatever you do, you must keep on asking yourself the question "what lessons can I draw from this which will be useful for my team, my peers and my superiors?"

Making the most of your time means moving your self-image away from that of a contributor to that of a teacher. And always remember the old proverb "if a student hasn't learned then the teacher hasn't taught". Spend time thinking about how you share these lessons, for that way you will also benefit from the other hackneyed but ever so true phrase "nobody ever forgets a great teacher".

STEP 2
VERTICAL
AGILITY

SHIFTING
HIGH AND LOW
TO MOVE UP

STEP-BY-STEP
WALKTHROUGH

If you stop to think about it, even for a minute, the dread experienced by anyone afraid of flying is inbuilt into the experience.

Who thought it would be a good idea to call the place you go to board a flight a "terminal"? Whoever declared that we should say "see you on the other side" when someone is about to board or go through "security"? Which genius decided that the first 5 minutes of every flight should be devoted to reminding you of everything that could possibly go wrong as you are about to defy the laws of physics (i.e. heavy must always fall)? Who trained the check-in agents to ask if the destination on your ticket is your "final destination"?

Words matter to anyone looking for reasons to be afraid.

Whether you fear flying or not, there are nevertheless some words that should warn you that you may want to avoid a hot cup of coffee on the flight. These words are normally uttered by the pilot at the start of the flight in that most calming of voices I suspect pilots are trained to adopt.

"Ladies and Gentlemen, after our climb we will take a right turn and continue to ascend to our cruising altitude of 24,000 feet for this short flight to …"

24,000 feet is the clue. Now if you're a metric person 24,000 feet means little to you in terms of height. I have been on enough flights however to know that "24,000 feet" means rodeo time. 24,000 feet is that little strip of no man's land towards the top of the cloud cover. It is that bouncy castle like layer where clouds come and go as fast as you go up and down. 24,000 feet means no hot drinks for me and a few stiff ones for others.

We have come to view our work life as a flight.

At the top, having reached the dizzying heights of executive leadership, sit the 39,000 feet people. As far as they can see the horizon is clear. The cloud cover hides the bumpy terrain, and everything is clear and sunny.

At 5,000 feet live the people for whom things are in focus. They can see what lies ahead and they make do with the terrain they inhabit. The clouds above may obstruct a grand vision but as long as they put one foot in front of the other they can still navigate the terrain.

And then come us, the 24,000 feet people, the ones experiencing the turbulence of being in the clouds. We know what "they" above want, even if they don't always articulate it that clearly. We also know what "they" below need, even if they struggle to realize it. Yet, somehow, we have to navigate a course in the turbulence that comes from balancing conflicting demands.

Whilst the analogy may capture the way you feel it also obscures the way you will succeed.

Great executives do not live at 39,000 feet any more than great employees spend their time at 5,000. And above all, given what we are trying to achieve here, you will never get the promotion you want or deserve if you're stuck at 24,000 feet. The key to becoming an executive lies in your ability to pilot the plane from bottom to top and back down again. Constantly. Consistently. Coherently. Safely. And at high speed.

This is what vertical agility is all about.

If boundless perspective is our ability to think about the forces impacting the organization, then vertical agility is "applied boundless perspective". It is about doing something. It is about being effective in our golden ratio of time spent IN, ON and OUT of the business.

Moving to executive level means managing a significant ramp up in the complexity, volume, breadth and potential impact of issues, as well as the timeframes associated with these. Paradoxically the impact of any decision in time is inversely proportionate to the time needed for the decision to be taken.

The variables are multiple and the consequences of wrong decisions catastrophic. The journey can be planned but the trip cannot be known. The time for action is immediate at a time when the consequences would warrant significant thinking. Against a context of shifting boundaries (or indeed in the absence of any boundaries at all), and with neither certainty nor control, leaders need to determine what needs to be done. And do so quickly.

The best way to lead is not from a control tower on the ground or a satellite at great height. The best way to lead is to be able to travel quickly between the ground and the sky to set a course that is both practical in the now and beneficial for the future. We need to pilot the plane with one eye on the horizon, and another on the instrument panel that indicates the status and positioning of the aircraft.

The leaders who are masters at this form of flying have the ability to cut through:

- the noise to identify what needs most attention as well as face up to totally unforeseen issues.
- the tensions and paradoxes that prevail in any decision to reach innovative and valuable outcomes.
- the perceived limitations of the organization as it is both run and changed at the same time.

There are some fundamental skills in mastering this characteristic. In part 2, I will tackle the following three questions, the answers to which are key to developing and displaying your mastery of vertical agility.

1. **How do I know when to act and when to stand back when there are so many variables and so much uncertainty?**

This question is really about where you position your plane.

When should you be working on the ground and when should you be flying high? What decisions should you make about your flight path?

You will never be right 100 percent of the time. You will do well if you are right half the time and luck is on your side for 20% of the time. In the words of a CEO client of mine, for the other 30% you will have to learn to forgive yourself. But there is one sure way to be wrong in the 80% of the time that is down to you rather than luck and that is to not make a decision at all.

To be fair, in the short to mid term, a large proportion of the way you will be judged as a leader will be down to the outcome of decisions taken by your predecessors. Such is life. But, your ability to make decisions that lead to action in the face of uncertainty and myriads of competing demands will determine your ability to retain the goodwill of your stakeholders.

So, the first question we will focus on in the next chapter is how do you make sure you operate at the right level to cut through the clouds and see clarity where others see fog at best and chaos at worst?

2.   How can I make a decision when there is no clear choice?

This is where the flying analogy really falls apart. Planes, by and large, are predictable. Everything has a function. When you push a button something happens, and if it doesn't happen there is a back-up for it. There are back-ups for everything because you know what you want to happen. Planes are 'if A then B' machines.

Organizations are not planes. If A, then B seldom works. Successful outcomes are not either/or propositions. There are advantages and disadvantages to every course of action open to you. There are tensions and trade-offs whatever course of action you take. Executives deal in a world of dilemmas.

So how will you deal with the trade-offs? How will you look to optimize as opposed to reduce? How can you use what some of our research executives have called lateral problem-solving and others, inductive thinking, to come up with decisions?

3.   How can I make decisions to change the organization for the long term whilst having to run it in the short term?

When you have a mechanism for decision-making as well as a mindset for breakthrough thinking you will invariably end up with this question.

Whether it is budget, capacity or capability there is always something in the current set up that will limit your ability to achieve your desired outcome. That's why start-ups find it so much easier to be innovative. They have nothing to lose.

It would be nice to ignore the short-term losses on the way to your innovative big win, but the short-term results are the only means to pay for your long-term goals so how do you change and run an organization at the same time?

This is the last question of vertical agility and the one you will need to answer successfully if you are to flourish as a leader.

So, ladies and gentlemen, please keep your seat belts fastened as we do here in the cockpit in case we encounter any unforeseen turbulence and as we move off on the runway to start our journey through vertical agility, let me wish you a pleasant flight!

9 THE THREE ROLES OF A LEADER – KNOWING WHAT TO DO AND WHEN TO STOP

QUESTION THIS CHAPTER WILL ANSWER
★
How do I decide what to act on, and when, for maximum impact?

Winnie the Pooh might not be your go-to management book but it has a lot to teach us.

In the first book we are introduced to the iconic bear when Christopher Robin, the little boy created by A.A. Milne, half awake, comes down the stairs in his pajamas, dragging it[9] along by the ear.

Don't worry - this is not an analogy about executive life suggesting you have to drag people along. The sentiment expressed by Winnie however is something every executive will be familiar with. It goes like this.

As his head bounces on each stair tread, Winnie is thinking to himself: There must be a better way to come down the stairs. There has to be. And if only my head could stop hurting for a second, I am sure I could even work out what this better way is.

----

9. It doesn't feel right somehow to use "it" to describe Winnie. So, with apologies to purists, I shall use the male pronoun henceforth if you don't mind!

And there you have it. How many times have you thought, "If only my head could stop hurting for a second I am sure I could find a better way? If only I had more time I could come up with a better solution. If only I'd had the resources it would have been different. If only I didn't have to sort A out, I could have taken care of B".

We are all Winnies.

I am pretty sure the good people at McKinsey didn't have Winnie the Pooh in mind when they came up with their 3 horizons model but if Winnie had had a consulting budget he could have found here a good conceptualization of his plight!

The model tells us that every organization must operate under 3 time horizons.

The 3 horizons model

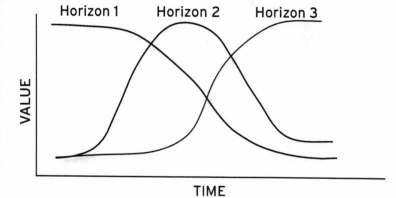

Horizon 1 is the now. It is about fulfilling immediate needs - flying the plane if you will, or indeed, working IN the business. It is valuable, but the value will decrease over time as the environment changes.

Horizon 3 is about the future. It is about the ultimate destination. It is about working OUT of the business. It is the "why". It is necessary because without a destination, activities are meaningless. It has huge future value but very little value in the now.

Horizon 2, as you might have guessed, is the middle one. It is about making the transition from now to tomorrow. It is about taking the business with you to a new place. It is our working ON the business.

This model explains why, as an executive, you have three roles, devoted in turn to achieving the objectives of leading a successful organization today, tomorrow and forever after.

The 3 roles of a leader

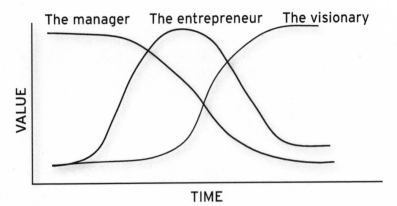

- **Role 1 - The manager**

I absolutely hate the endless debates about the difference between management and leadership. I just don't care what the answer is. Life is too short, and you need both so get over it. 'Manager' in this context however is a useful word.

One job of the executive is to manage the work today. It is not to do all the work yourself, but it is to ensure that your sleeves are sufficiently rolled up so that what must be delivered is delivered.

- **Role 3 - The visionary**

I am not talking Steve Jobs (or whomever you have in mind as a visionary) here. I am simply talking about the job of knowing where you want to take your business. You have to have a vision for it. Your vision doesn't have to be grand (i.e. we will save the world by doing x) but it has to be real.

Every organization is struggling for a noble cause these days. It seems de rigueur to have one given we are constantly told people do not work for a salary but for purpose. It will be for you to judge whether your cause is noble (by way of a tip here, the more it is true the more noble it is likely to be) but you must have a vision. You must have a view as to how your market will change and what you will be in that changed market. That's what I mean by visionary.

- **Role 2 – The entrepreneur**

Some might use the word "intrapreneur" here, but I just don't like it. It feels clumsy and a bit like consultant jargon to me, so I'll stick to entrepreneur.

This is the job that alone justifies your salary. You can get away with outsourcing the role of visionary. It's a commodity - an expensive commodity depending on which strategy house you use but a commodity nevertheless. I am not dismissing the role but just saying that you can get cover for it.

You can get away with not being the best manager if you have the best people. If the machine you inherit when you get promoted is in good shape, it will run itself for some time with just some minor servicing needed along the way.

What won't happen on its own though - irrespective of how you're set up, is the organization shifting from where it is today to where it needs to be tomorrow. That's the job of the entrepreneur. That's why we have executives and that's why we pay them like executives.

What we mean when we talk about vertical agility is the ability to do all three roles at once. It is about you having the resilience and agility to move quickly between the three and use what you see in each to benefit your input in the others.

If you want to make the grade you have to add value and be seen to do so. So here is our first key question:

How do I decide what to act on, and when, for maximum impact?

Well we already know what you need to think about because we covered this earlier under the boundless perspective banner. Remember it's all about the IN/ON/OUT. I described Vertical Agility as "applied" Boundless Perspective in so far as it is about putting our insights to work.

Now for simplification we can assume that Role 1 (manager) is about working IN, 2 (entrepreneur) is about working ON and 3 (visionary) is about working OUT. We can make this assumption, but we shouldn't overplay it. In fact, in practice, you can only excel in any of these roles if you work at all three levels but at this stage the main thing to worry about is how do we navigate between the three. That is to say how do we know when to be up and when to be down?

The answer to the question is pretty much always dictated by events. We may like to think about the life of an executive being about the execution of a strategy, but it is mainly about keeping a plan on track. It is much more tactical than it is strategic due to events.

Let's take some examples. Someone comes to your desk and tells you something has gone wrong in one of your plants. Will you be working as a manager, entrepreneur or visionary? You open the papers and see that the regulator is planning some new rules for one of your key products. Will you tackle this as a manager, entrepreneur or visionary? You're preparing for an investor roadshow. Are you a manager, entrepreneur or visionary?

The truth is that, in all three scenarios, you have all three roles.

First, you must do the work (do something to get the plant issue fixed, talk to legal and marketing about the regulation and get the presentation straight).

Second, you must do the work that will get you closer to your stated vision (Are we solving the problem at the plant in line with our values? Is the new regulation likely to impact the way we do business? What messages do we need to convey to our investors and what actions do we want them to take?).

Finally, you must do the work that will get you closer to your stated vision in a way that builds foundations for the future (Can we learn something about what happened at the plant that will stop this happening in the future? Should we build closer relationships with the regulator to shape the agenda? Is the way we handle our relationships with shareholders and analysts the best it can be?).

Playing all three roles at once is what Vertical Agility is about. It is possible as long as you have a disciplined and ordered approach to each and every event. Vertical Agility is a deliberate act.

Events, Responses and Outcomes

The problem with events is that they tend to bring with them pressure and pressure makes us go into autopilot. I promise this is the last (well maybe the penultimate) time I will use the flying analogy. When an incident occurs on a flight, pilots respond instinctively. Years of training, drills, studying checklists and virtual rehearsals have turned their responses into reflexes. They do what they are trained to do and do it well. Their response is almost instinctive. Their limbs move without any noticeable thinking.[10]

The same is true of you. Unless you have had years of experience as an executive the likelihood is that events will dictate a non-executive response. You are less likely to move up and down in your response and more likely to stay focused on what you know how to do.

The common response and common mistake is to witness an event and then react to create an outcome. What the ancient Greek stoic philosophers postulated, neuroscience has now proven – it is our interpretation of events rather than the events themselves that dictate our response thereby predicting the outcome. In his bestselling book 'The Success Principles', author Jack Canfield formulates this as an elegant equation $E+R=O$ where E is the event, O the outcome and R our response. When it comes to unleashing your inner leader however, your focus should be on the R. The key to practicing Vertical Agility is to break out of our normal reactions and learn to target our response. The key to executive success is to see the equation as $E + r/R=O$ where the choice between r for react and R for respond will determine your success.

---

10. There is in fact plenty of thinking going on. If you are interested in understanding the different ways our brains tackle the task of thinking you should get hold of Daniel Kehneman's seminal work 'Thinking, Fast and Slow' which as well as being fascinating is a demonstration that you can be a Nobel Prize winner and still make your subject approachable.

Here is the last reference to flying and I'll make it about landing so that it signals the end of the analogy and does so in a tidy way!

Imagine you have landed after a long flight. You just want to get home. The plane was delayed, and you had to wait ages for the gate. You're a really nice person but right now you don't feel like one. You reach immigration and as usual the line stretching in front of you resembles the worst of Disneyland at school vacation time without the popcorn and the fun.

Out of the 20 counters only 4 are manned. That's bad. But to make matters worse, you can see a couple of immigration agents, chatting away with seemingly not a care in the world while they enjoy cups of coffee.

So here is the event E.

Now you have an option. You can respond (R) or you can react (r).

A reaction will look something like this. You get more and more worked up. You eventually reach the counter and make some derogatory comment about the poor quality of service. Depending on the country in which you have landed this could lead to anything from a feedback form to a custodial sentence being handed out to you!

A response on the other hand may well be something like this. You reach the counter and say "I tell you what I feel so stressed having queued for an hour I just don't know how you cope with doing this all day, every day. They don't even seem to give you much of a break away from it all having to stand there to have a cup of coffee rather than get the chance to go somewhere quiet".

My guess is that in this scenario the interaction is likely to be both more pleasant and potentially shorter as the person at the desk sends you on your way with an approving smile.

The point is that the way you respond or react will dictate the outcome you get.

Vertical agility requires choosing the R over the r and getting the sequencing Event, Response and Outcome in the right order.

$$E + r/R = O$$

As our example illustrates it is the event and your response to it that will define the outcome.

In life in general and with Vertical Agility in particular, it is always better to respond (R) than to react (r). Yet, the more tired and pressured we feel, the less self-control we exhibit. Given everything we know about the relationship leaders have with time we can hazard a guess that pressure and tiredness are likely to feature frequently in your decision-making processes. The more you progress, the more R risks regressing to r. How do you then ensure you choose R over r? What is the trick to applying the self-control necessary to making the right choice?

The answer lies in the order you choose to focus on each of the variables in the $E + r/R = O$ equation.

1. Get to know everything there is to know about the E

You must first think about the E. What do you know about the event? Have you got all the information you need? Can you go beyond the obvious and behind the scenes? In our airport event above, you actually know very little. Maybe the officers chatting over their coffees were discussing how to reduce the line? Maybe they were actively gathering intelligence to protect you? Maybe they were just on a break because they had been working non-stop for too long and their effectiveness was compromised? Who knows? Well you should.

Get to know everything there is to know about the E and don't let your wish to react interfere with your ability to gather data.

2. Then comes the O.

The difference between a reaction and a response is the amount of time you have spent thinking about the outcome you want.

Surely the outcome you wanted at the airport was to get home as quickly as possible. If you had thought about that, even for a split second, you would have realized that a confrontation with an immigration officer at an arrival gate was never the strategy most likely to deliver your desired outcome.

Focusing on the O will not only give you some idea as to what to do - it will also give you the time to calm down and so avoid the r.

3. Finally go for the R

Armed with full knowledge of the event and a clear view of the outcome you seek, you can now choose a response. The R is actually the only element of decision-making you have complete control over. You can't do anything about the event given it has happened and there will be many variables that will impact the outcome, but the R is entirely down to you, so you owe it to yourself to spend time planning for it.

Your success in displaying Vertical Agility rests in your ability to give the R at the right level. Think through the three roles of a leader - are you sure your response takes all three into account?

One last word on what you need to do and when you need to do it. None of the above should be tackled alone. In the last part of the book we will come back to the importance of teams and how to build one that works, but needless to say that gathering data on an event, defining an outcome and planning a response is always best done with others' input. You don't have to outsource the decision-making power, but you will always do better with the right input.

You must focus on the immediate, mid and long term and you now know how to ensure that you respond accordingly to the events you face. However, there is one more issue with Vertical Agility. When you do the work above you will quickly realize that most of the situations you face will not be either/or situations but rather 'and' situations where the two propositions on each side of the 'and' appear opposite yet desirable. Let's turn to the next chapter to work out how you can reconcile the dilemmas and tension that are the essence of executive decision-making.

RECAP

Succeeding at Vertical Agility requires you to know what to focus on and to be able to make decisions in ambiguity.

When it comes to knowing what to focus on, there are three roles that a leader should fulfill.

- Role 1 - the manager – this is about ensuring you deliver today
- Role 2 – the entrepreneur – this is about being able to move your business from today to tomorrow
- Role 3 – the visionary – this is about articulating a course with a clear destination of where you are taking the business and why.

We have already spoken about how you can get the information necessary to fulfill these roles with our IN/ON/OUT model. The trick now is to understand how you move seamlessly between the three.

This is where the $E + r/R = O$ method comes in.

An outcome (the O) is always a function of your response (the R) to an event (the E).

The main variable for us to focus on to determine the O is our R. The trick is not to confuse Respond (R) with react (r). Reacting is unplanned. It is instinctive. Responding is planned. It is thoughtful.

To ensure you remain focused on adding value and work at the right level you need to fully understand the E, decide on your O and plan your Response. What you should never do, is react (r) to an Event. This leaves the outcome to chance.

This may sound easy, but it takes an enormous amount of self-awareness and self-control.

10 MOVING BEYOND "EITHER/ORS" TO CREATE BREAKTHROUGHS

QUESTIONS THIS CHAPTER WILL ANSWER ★

How do I ensure that only what deserves my focus gets to my desk?

How do I deal with the inherent tensions of executive decision-making?

"I really worry when I have to make an easy decision."

This was the view of a CEO I was discussing decision-making with. In his world, if a decision was an easy one, someone else should have made it long before it reached his desk.

His is a world of hard decisions, trade-offs, dilemmas and tensions. His role, as he sees it, is not to be a decision maker: he is an arbiter of tough choices. If he is asked to make easy decisions, something must be broken somewhere in the organization.

That's an executive view of decision-making and it's a view that requires Vertical Agility.

The executive role is not just a decision-making role. It is a role that requires a focus on two particular aspects of decision-making.

The first is to build capability in the organization to minimize decision-making being escalated. If decisions can only be made at executive level the organization is paralyzed.

The second is to build your own capability to deal with the tensions and dilemmas that arrive on your desk.

Let's take each in turn.

How do I ensure that only what deserves my focus gets to my desk?

Let's turn back to the $E + R/r = O$ model we looked at in the previous chapter.

Of course, in all situations, you want your employees to respond rather than react to any event. To do so however they need to be clear about the outcome they are aiming for. Clarity is key. In most cases, their accountabilities will be clear on the desired outcome of their action, their - performance agreement tells them what they should aim for. There are times however when things are not that clear.

Take the example of a performer at one of Disney's parks around the world. Their accountability is clear – make the show the greatest it can be. That's it. Be in the moment the best you can be to make the show something people will remember forever. That's pretty clear and unambiguous.

Now imagine yourself being one of these performers. Whilst doing your Tigger act (or whatever other act you've always dreamt of performing - I don't want to be overly prescriptive here), you spot a child crying in the audience. He looks lost.

What would you do? You know what your accountability is. The show must go on. Now you find yourself conflicted. You know the show must go on but you also know a child crying doesn't seem to add up to the kind of memories you are supposed to create.

You have a dilemma.

Disney knows however that this is a dilemma that many a performer will face during many a performance, so they have an answer to help you. They call the answer one of the Disney Keys. Yes, the show is key but actually, in all instances, courtesy is even more important than the show. So, there you go - you must help the child. Job done. Outcome secured. Event faced. Right response achieved.

Now imagine that you have moved to one of the rides and some teenagers are refusing to fasten their seatbelts. What do you do? You've asked politely three times to no avail. You're ready to eject them from the ride but you remember that courtesy is even more important than the show - yet another dilemma and yet another key. Disney is clear. Safety trumps courtesy and the show.

Like all good keys, the Disney keys unlock decision-making. They ensure that regardless of the complexity of the event, the right outcome is achieved through the right response.

Vertical Agility demands that executives understand how the smallest of decisions can be aligned to the highest of aims. This is achieved by minutely devising planned outcomes and responses to predictable events that cut across accountabilities.

The idea is to determine an order of importance in the legitimate demands you make.

Of course, sometimes it will be impossible to order demands. On occasion, A will be as important as B. When this is the case, another way to achieve the goal of enabling clarity of response is 'phasing'.

Phasing works by determining what comes first. Yes, both A and B are as important as each other but right now we will do A before we move on to B. Providing this is a genuine strategy and the phasing does occur (as opposed to being a way to kick a decision into the long grass), this is another acceptable strategy to dealing with dilemmas.

What both require is a depth of understanding of how the organization works at every level and how information travels around each level. It requires the low level flying skills of vertical agility.

What are the dilemmas your team faces repeatedly which you could order or phase? How do you find out the dilemmas that other teams face as a result of the actions of your team?

These are questions you should be asking yourself now. Boundless Perspective helped you scan for pain points. Vertical Agility should help you solve them. The more you help people around you address the dilemmas they face, the more you will be perceived as the person with the keys.

There are however dilemmas that are just that - two propositions of equal legitimacy and value that cannot be ordered or phased. In fact, most of these are built into the very fabric of organizational design. They are what my good friend and global authority on culture and management, Fons Trompenaars, calls OOH/OOH propositions for On the One Hand, On the Other Hand. This is where the second question comes in.

How do I deal with the inherent tensions of executive decision-making?

Should your organization design be global or local? Do you want to drive profitability or growth? Are you leading for the short term or the long term?

Putting your MBA hat aside, there is only one correct answer to these questions. The right answer is "both".

Up to now in your career you have been able to blame "they". When you couldn't do something it was because "they didn't let you". When you didn't have clarity it was because "they didn't know or understand". It was because "they couldn't make up their minds". The problem is if you want to become a senior leader you become "they". When people say "they…", they will mean you.

So, will you be too stupid to make up your mind or will you make up your mind never to be stupid? The second strategy is a lot more likely to get you to success[11].

This may seem a bit overly philosophical; after all, events may well dictate an outcome. You may decide that the most appropriate response to the local versus global dilemma, in current circumstances, is to go local. You may try to phase the answer. However, there is something much more interesting when you replace "either/or" with "and" - you get the agility to create breakthroughs. Let me walk you through an example.

You are leading a production team in a bottling plant and you have been asked to attend a meeting with the marketing team. The marketing team is pushing to increase the number of bottle types

---

11. For more information on this type of integrative or through-through thinking you can read any of Fons Trompenaars' marvelously witty and well written books (start with 'Did the Pedestrian Die?'), or alternatively, take a look at Roger Martin's superb 'The Opposable Mind'.

going through your plant. Of course, for ease of production you would like one bottle type. They, however, reckon that having 400 would be a whole lot better because it would help them target very specific consumer segments. What's the right number of bottles to have?

I'm sure you will have attended similar meetings where your accountabilities have seemed to clash with those of others. If they are anything like the ones I have attended in my career, they are painfully predictable. Everyone argues. People do not so much stay quiet to listen, but rather to reload their next argument.

That is until, for the sake of decorum and getting home on time, everyone agrees on 200 bottle types and we move on. All is good until the next meeting when everything will be up for grabs again.

Now imagine being the CEO of the company and getting a knock on your office door (or someone walks straight in because you have an open door policy). You find in front of you both the head of production and the head of marketing. They ask, "Boss do you want maximum production efficiency or maximum segment penetration?". What's your answer? It's got to be "both", of course.

That's the dilemma. So how do you come up with a solution which is not the 200-bottle compromise that achieves nothing?

The key is to rephrase the question and change your thinking. The question is not either/or; it is not a continuum from 1 to 400 bottles. The question is: how does having the maximum efficiency of 1 bottle help us have maximum penetration of 400 segments? Or how can having 400 bottles help us be more efficient. The answer is not on a line but in the upper right-hand side quadrant of a 2 by 2 where one axis is number of bottles and the other is number of segments.

Breaking the line of dilemmas

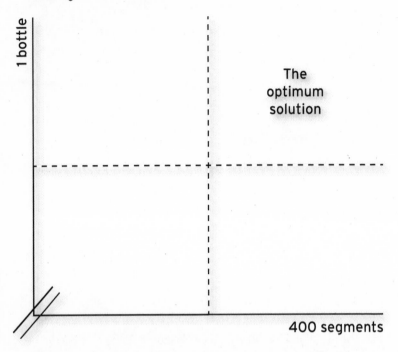

I know it sounds confusing (after all one of my clients described himself as being "at first, as confused as a chameleon on a packet of Smarties" in a discussion with Fons and I on dilemma reconciliation). But the point is that you need to apply what can only be described as "through/through" thinking.

It's not "should we be local or global?" but rather "how can being global help us be even more local and vice versa?". It shouldn't be "are we aiming for the short term or long term?" but rather "how can acting short term secure our long term and vice versa?". It cannot possibly be "do you want growth or profitability?"...you get the idea.

At the very least when you rephrase the question the discussion changes. By asking "how can having one bottle help us target 400 segments?" or "how can having 400 bottles help us be more efficient?", you change the dynamics of the conversation. As a result, you are much more likely to end up with innovative solutions rather than destructive compromises.

This is why Vertical Agility is such a key differentiator in executive roles as for this type of thinking to occur you need to change the working dynamics at every level of the organization. You need to ensure that every issue is depersonalized and made emotionally neutral. Ask people to list all the disadvantages and advantages of each position and then ask them to see how they can use the positives of one to reinforce the positives of the other.

If you do this you may well discover that far from being a bottle issue, maybe you need to think about labeling or the way the plant is organized or whatever else the people who know about these things can come up with. That's the key here. What you want to happen is that people who know about these things come together with open minds and inquisitive brains to generate breakthrough solutions.

What you don't want is for them to blame "they" for setting unrealistic targets.

Vertical Agility is about creating clarity of work as well as clarity of outcomes. It is about being able to act at the right level to move the organization forward. Your role therefore is ensuring that those around you understand.

The biggest difference you can make today to begin demonstrating this leadership characteristic is to stop colluding with the organizational mindset of "they". You cannot and will never become a senior leader unless you become "they" and there is nothing to stop you doing it now.

The easiest way to start is with your team by simply drawing a two by two on a flipchart before you start discussions that you know are filled with dilemmas (especially cross-functional ones) and ask, "how do we get to the top right-hand quadrant?". You may never get there but you will have had some of the most constructive conversations you have experienced in a long time. And if you do get there you will discover that the top right-hand quadrant is where breakthrough ideas live and breakthrough products, services and business models are developed.

The biggest tension of all and the biggest challenge when it comes to Vertical Agility is: how do you run an organization today but get it future ready at the same time? How do you change by staying put? Being able to deal with this last challenge of Vertical Agility will not only differentiate you as an aspiring executive but also ensure you succeed when you get there. So, let's turn our attention to this issue next.

RECAP

Vertical Agility is having the ability to make tough calls when decisions involve trade-offs and dilemmas in a way that not only helps the organization move forward but also builds capability and clarity at all levels.

To do so means mastering two complementary disciplines.

The first is what we call 'ordering and phasing'. This is when, having reviewed your strategic imperatives along with their multiple "on the ground" implications, you are able to form a hierarchy of needs or a phasing for achievement in time.

The second is what we think of as dilemma reconciliation. This is when, having discovered that you are faced with two equally desirable yet seemingly opposite propositions, you look at ways in which you can combine them by using the positives from one to reinforce the other.

You can develop this key component of Vertical Agility by focusing on the pain points you discovered using Boundless Perspective. Gather all the data you can on these from every level of the organization. Bring together a disparate group of people from multiple areas affected. Facilitate a conversation aiming to use the positives on each side of the problem to reinforce each other. Armed with this new type of thinking you will stage generative discussions that can deliver breakthrough solutions.

11 THE CAPABILITY MINDSET – RUNNING AND CHANGING AN ORGANIZATION AT ONCE

QUESTIONS THIS CHAPTER WILL ANSWER ★

How do you set up an approach to running and changing your organization at the same time?

How do you get your team to understand the importance of both?

"We don't have a green field site. We know what we need. We know what to do. But each and every day we have to use our resources fixing what we have, in order to maintain what we need, so we can fund what we want."

How do you get to the place where you want to be whilst having to spend all your time defending the place you have? How do you go forward whilst having to stand still?

The CTO who gave me the quote above fights each and every day to make the financial institution he works for the best it can be right now, yet he knows that doing so won't make it the best it needs to be for the future.

He is not stupid. He is not lazy. He does not have yesterday's mindset unable to face up to the Fintech upstarts. In fact, what the quote doesn't reflect is the solution he has come up with to the executive problem of running and changing an organization at once.

This solution is the one I want to share with you to help you make the impact you need to make to get the executive job you seek. This solution I call "the capability mindset".

In many ways squaring this circle is the culmination of everything we have covered so far.

Your Boundless Perspective has helped you deepen your understanding of where you are and where you want to go.

Moving the company from today to tomorrow is the role of the entrepreneur that we identified as a key role of executives.

The E+r/R=O equation has helped you reframe your responses to events so that you can exert more control over their outcomes.

The integrative mindset of phasing/prioritizing and dilemma reconciliation gives you an approach to the issue of delivering short-term whilst preparing for the long term.

So what does the capability mindset offer you? In short, it is a methodology that enables you to identify the filters to apply to issues (long term versus short term, growth versus productivity, facts versus judgment).

It enables you to judge effectively when it is best to rise above the detail but also where digging much deeper is essential.

It helps you identify when something is suboptimal.

It is a map to guide you in fulfilling the right leadership role at the right time to maximize value in a sustainable way.

Running the company whilst simultaneously changing is the same dilemma as short-term versus long-term thinking. The way to solve this dilemma is to change both your mindset as well as your organization culture.

Success depends on you being able to answer two questions:

- How do I set up an approach to both running and changing my organization at the same time?

- How do I get my team to understand the importance of both running the organization today, whilst also changing it to make it future-fit?

Let's take each in turn.

The capability mindset

What our CTO advocates is recognition that today and tomorrow are never separate. Running the company and changing it are not challenges you can phase over time. Both are needed, and both are needed today – irrespective of your resources.

Whatever you do today will either help or hinder you in your future quest. What you do today in an organization will either help or hinder your future earnings. Whatever happens today will either produce the results to support the journey towards tomorrow or lead to the underperformance that will remove your right to continue.

What the capability mindset advocates is that you need to think of today's effort not as something that detracts from tomorrow's success, but rather as steps to building tomorrow.

Running the business and changing it are the inescapable "whats" of your role. The capability mindset is about a complete focus on the "how".

Today's results are necessary and need to be achieved. Tomorrow's strategic imperatives are real and will need to be reached. Your success lies in understanding HOW what you do today helps or hinders what you do tomorrow.

The capability mindset is what links running the business to changing this. It ensures that your response to events adds value today and tomorrow.

The capability mindset link

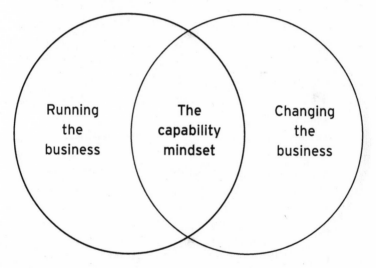

Here is how it works.

When evaluating any strategic imperative or option (i.e. changing the business), ask yourself these two questions:

- What capabilities will we need to deliver this outcome?
- How can we use what we do today to develop these capabilities?

When facing any operational task or decision (i.e. running the business), ask yourself these two questions:

- How can this task be used to change the organization?
- How can I use this task to help me develop the future capabilities we need?

In effect, our CTO is using the "through/through" mindset we advocated in the previous chapter. Keeping these four questions front of mind is helping him make practical the proposition "how can running the business help me change it and how can changing it help me run it better".

Thinking capability first helps him move forward. It avoids the risk of standing still whilst fixing issues today.

Thinking capability first helps him get closer to tomorrow. The capability mindset means always looking for answers to these questions:

- Are we learning some new skills today that we know we will need tomorrow?
- Can I use what we do today as an opportunity to talk to the team about where we want to get to tomorrow, so they can come up with an approach that fixes today in a way that moves us forward faster?

The capability mindset is what the entrepreneur role is about, and what working ON the business is. It is why the magic ratio we talked about in Boundless Perspective is so skewed towards working ON the business.

What is important to note, and our CTO is at pains to point out, is that the capability mindset approach can only work if your entire team has a capability culture.

The capability culture

Let's be clear here - having a capability mindset is not easy when tenure and rewards all point to the short term. However, your job is to continue providing clarity at all times; and to reinforce the importance of capability building for today, tomorrow and forever after. Your success will depend on creating a capability culture.

To make this happen you will need to adopt four habits that, together, will help you focus your team on the delivery of sustainable results.

Of course, they are not meant to replace the non-negotiable basics we have already established you possess in chapter 1. However, used alongside these, they will ensure you build the kind of culture that will support you in your endeavors.

1.   Make the run/change agenda overt

The first thing to do is to ensure that your team is aware of the importance of acting for both today and tomorrow at once. Don't use the short-term vs. long-term dichotomy. It doesn't help as it forces prioritizing. Most people would rather forget about tomorrow. They agree with economist John Maynard Keynes' famous phrase "in the long term we're all dead".

Instead, reiterate your vision of the future and explain that "how" you go about delivering today will determine whether you achieve your vision or not.

I can't overstate the importance of this step. Not only does it establish a culture of sustainable delivery and keep the beat of your business going, but it also positions you in the minds of the leaders around you as an executive in waiting.

One practical way to do this is to conduct two meetings where you previously had one. Have a running the business meeting (focused on results) and a changing the business meeting (focused on capability).

Whilst it may appear to reinforce the divide, in practice this gives both agendas equal importance. It sounds crazy, and it is, but people will always try to ascribe priorities on the basis of your actions (we will get back to that when we talk about Steadfast Impact). If you only have one meeting to cover both and start it with running the business and conclude with changing it others will infer from this that you care about today's results more! By having two meetings you ensure people know you care about both equally.

2. Manage for capability and lead for results

When it comes to how you spend your time go back to the three roles of a leader.

To manage effectively today you should have already ensured you have people around you who you trust to deliver. Whether you have direct reports who manage teams, or you have a team yourself to manage doesn't matter. You need to set the goal and let them get on with it, trusting that they have what it takes to deliver.

Your role is to manage capability. You have to ask, over and over again, the four questions of the capability mindset:
- What capabilities will we need to deliver this outcome?
- How can we use what we do today to develop these capabilities?
- How can this task be used to change the organization?
- How can I use this task to help me develop the future capabilities we need?

Trust that your team knows what actions to take (and if you don't trust them, do something about this) and question relentlessly the capability these actions build.

3. Do your knitting

I don't mean stick to your knitting and keep on doing what you're good at; instead I mean ensure that at all times you stitch running and changing the business together in your own mind and those of the people around you. The key, again, and I make no apologies for being repetitive, is to focus on capabilities.

The role of the entrepreneur is to ensure that whatever happens today gets us closer to what we want tomorrow. The role of the executive entrepreneur is to ensure that everybody is aware of this. So, in everything you do and everything you say you must think, say and do "capability first".

Remind people of the need for sustainable and capability - generative results. Measure it, discuss it and include it in all your communications.

4. Keep your varifocal glasses on at all times

Events do and will happen, and they will require a response. Your response cannot be a reaction, but neither should it be a lack of action.

There are times when you will have to do something to run the business that you had not planned to do. They may require you to put aside some of the activities or investments you had planned to change the business. The two worst reactions you can have are either to jump in and forget about changing the business or to refuse to do anything now if it damages your business change plans.

Remember the capability mindset and go back to the four capability questions. The key is can we use this event to learn something different from what we had planned. The difference between achieving your goal and not achieving it is not failure but rather the opportunity to ask, "what do we know now that we didn't know when we set this objective/target?"

Being opportunistic in responding to events is the sign of great entrepreneurship.

Thinking about capability as the link between running and changing the business is fundamentally about how you, as an executive, can impact the organization.

Impact is what leadership is all about and executive roles need to exert a very different kind of impact.

It is the third of our unique characteristics of senior leadership roles and the one we turn to now in our next and final step to getting you match fit for executive promotion.

RECAP

The need for Vertical Agility is not felt anywhere more acutely than when you have to tackle the biggest executive challenge, namely, how to run and change the organization at the same time.

The key to doing so is to have the right mindset and build a culture inside the organization where people share this mindset.

Having the right mindset means you must relentlessly focus on capability.

The capability mindset

Having a capability mindset is about recognizing that whatever you do today is not separate from what you will get tomorrow and vice versa. It is about having the ability to think about what you do today as an opportunity to build sustainable results that deliver your vision.

In practice it is about linking the work you do today to the strategic vision you have for the organization through capabilities. It is about viewing every operational action and strategic decision through the lens of four questions:

- What capabilities will we need in the future to deliver our strategy?
- How can we use what we do today to develop these capabilities?
- How can this task we have to complete today to run the organization be used to change it?
- How can I use this task to help me develop the future capabilities we need?

Ensuring that those around you see the need both to act in the now but also to act sustainably requires you to build a capability culture

The capability culture

To do this you will need to make the link overt between the needs of today and the needs of tomorrow. You will need to avoid giving priorities to these as they are intrinsically linked. Make sure they get equal time and share of attention. Make sure you link everything that happens to the capability it builds for the long term. Failure to do so will end up in you missing the opportunity to fulfill a key role of any leader – that of the entrepreneur.

STEP 3
STEADFAST
IMPACT

CHANGING YOUR IMPACT WHILST STAYING INTACT

12 STEP-BY-STEP WALKTHROUGH

Have you ever been to a gym?

Putting aside the fact that executive leadership requires the kind of stamina and resilience that comes with being healthy, if you've never been to one, you may want to visit a local gym and stand on a wobble board (also known as a balance board).

A wobble board is a simple piece of gym equipment. Think of it as a circular board with half a football underneath.

The aim of the wobble board is to help athletes build their core strength by balancing on the unsteady board.

Just like athletes, leaders have to learn to stand on a wobble board too in order to gain the core strength necessary to achieve[12].

The leadership wobble board comprises the needs of multiple stakeholders:
- The finance community made up of owners, shareholders, analysts etc.
- The customers/consumers of your products and services
- The suppliers (which also includes the people who supply your license to operate such as regulators, NGOs, journalists etc).
- The employees who work with you.

....

12. The leadership wobble board idea comes from our friend Shaun O'Callaghan with whom we have the good fortune to partner on some assignments. His book '*turnaround leadership*' is a must-read.

At any point in time their needs and demands will be different. They will often be seemingly incompatible. Your customers may well want your product for free, but your employees and suppliers will demand payment. The role of the leader is to keep the board balanced in order to achieve.

Everyone in the organization has a wobble board of some kind.

You may not have any direct interactions with shareholders or owners, but you still have to balance their demands, by way of a budget, against the demands of your team or your customers. You may not deal closely with customers but, in some ways, their needs will still impact the demands made of you.

There are two things that differentiate a senior leadership wobble board from any others in the organization.

- **The first is the sheer number, and instances, of people kicking your board whilst you are trying to balance.**

You could argue that the more senior you get, the further you are from the day-to-day running of the business. That being said, the more senior you get, the closer you are to the outcome of the thousands of actions taken by thousands of people every second of every day. You may well be the last to know if something goes wrong for any of the constituencies on the board, but that won't stop you from being the first to be asked about it.

As an executive you become the face of the organization. Yours is the go-to email address when things are not as they should be.

Your own wobble board is arguably the sum total of everyone else's. At the very least, whatever forces impact their boards will be amplified by the time they hit yours.

- **The second characteristic of the executive wobble board is that you are not the only one standing on it.**

Your executive team stands alongside you in trying to balance. Move one way all at once and the whole team risks falling off. Ignore one corner of the board and the forces impacting it become unmanageable.

Building your core strength is hard enough. Having to put up with relentless kicks to the board from stakeholders is tiresome enough. Having to do both whilst at the same time trying to compensate for the lack of, or overly felt, weight of others on the board can feel overwhelmingly impossible.

This is why everyone in our research mentioned the relentless nature of the executive role. It is an always-on role. However varied the audience, however unpredictable their demands, however unforeseen the circumstances, you have to respond. You have to balance. You have to impact.

We call this characteristic 'Steadfast Impact' to capture both the breadth of the constituencies who must be impacted as well as the need to balance their demands. Steadfast impact is in effect, your core executive strength. Mastering this characteristic is about being able to answer two questions.

1. **How do I maintain some semblance of authenticity if all of these people want something different and contradictory?**

You can't survive by just saying whatever you think people want to hear. It wouldn't help you get anywhere, never mind balance your board. You can't just be slick. You can't just post some snazzy quote on a social media site. You have to offer true leadership with real substance.

This demands both enormous energy and incredible persistence. It requires a strong moral and social compass to enable you to demonstrate consistently the values of the organization you lead - in all circumstances, in all environments and for all constituencies.

It requires clarity of mission and language.

2. How do I build a team around me who will support me in balancing the board?

You can't be an executive without managing politics. Arguably the very experience of being human is a struggle if you can't manage politics.

Put two people in a room together and politics happen. Social creatures are political creatures. You must manage the relationships around the executive table to balance your wobble board.

You will need to be absolutely clear about when and how best to make a contribution as a leader built on a strong understanding of the political landscape and dynamics.

You must have a foundation of rapid and honest feedback to manage the issues and conflicts that invariably arise when you put strong people together around a table.

In the following chapters we will work together to explore how successful executives respond to these challenges. I will offer you ways of thinking and techniques to help you cope with the always-on nature of the executive role and develop the required resilience to get through it.

The way we will do this is by tackling the need for Steadfast Impact in three phases (one per chapter).

If Steadfast Impact is about being true to your message when under pressure, we had better start by working out what your message is. We will look at how to find your executive voice as well as the techniques that can help you keep that voice confident and strong when the going gets tough. We will work out how to build your core executive strength so as to stay balanced even when strong forces are pushing and pulling on your board.

We will then look at how you can adapt your message to different constituencies whilst remaining authentic and consistent in your message. We will look at how you can impact each constituency differently using the same message rather than having to compromise or change this to make it fit.

Finally, we will turn to the executive team to understand why dysfunctions are both a blessing and a curse. I will share with you a very simple but powerful method to evaluate where best, and how to make a noted and strong impact at the top table despite politics and pressures.

Steadfast Impact is the unique characteristic we tackle last for a reason. It is the one you need to have at the forefront of your mind. It is the one you can't forget about. It is also an expression of the leadership mindset the other two have helped you develop. Mastering 'Boundless Perspective' and 'Vertical Agility' are prerequisites to having an impact that is worth making. Now let's look at something that is not remotely as easy at it sounds – how to be yourself!

13 MIRROR AND WINDOWS – FINDING YOUR LEADERSHIP VOICE IN ORDER TO BE HEARD

QUESTIONS THIS CHAPTER WILL ANSWER ★
How do I find out what I stand for?
How do I know what my varied audiences need from me?

Being a leader is all about the difference you can make, the decisions you take, the actions you complete and the value you create. It's all about impact.

You are questioned by your staff, interviewed by journalists, challenged by regulators and accosted by strangers in shopping centers. All have different questions and expectations.

The pressure is always on and the light shines bright on you.

It's easy in such an environment to believe that being a leader is all about you.

Yet, as a Finance Director we spoke to during the research for this book told us: "It's easy to be fooled. But, in all the instances you mention, whether I am successful or not has very little to do with me. It has everything to do with them".

He wasn't trying to make excuses or blame outcomes on someone else. I know people are fond of saying that executives are always quick to accept credit for great results and to allocate blame for poor ones but that's not what he was talking about. What he meant was that it doesn't really matter what you think you have done. What matters is what others experience and their experience is entirely down to them.

You may think that you have been clear but unless your audience also feels this way, you haven't been! You may think of yourself as honest and trustworthy but unless they agree, then to all intents and purposes, you're not.

The challenge for many aspiring executives is that to have Steadfast Impact you have to have something to say. This needs to be both consistent (otherwise you lose credibility) and also different (otherwise you have no impact). They normally phrase this challenge as a question. "How can I be authentic if I am different with everyone I meet?" Or they throw down the gauntlet: "Well you may not like it but I am just being authentic".

Mirror and windows

The way to master Steadfast Impact is to think about "mirror and windows".

The mirror is all about you. It is about having a core set of values, or a consistent truth, to share. You must be clear about your own drivers, preferences, habits and the messages you want to send. You have to know what you stand for, as well as the filters and habits you use when you respond to your environment. The mirror underpins your credibility and therefore your impact.

The windows are the filters you look through to understand others. To paint pictures they can relate to, you must have a clear and deep understanding of your intended targets' needs, desires, expectations and reactions. Having clear, open windows underpins the effectiveness of your impact.

Steadfast Impact is using your self- (mirror) and social-awareness (windows) as a springboard to craft strategies that are differentiated yet consistent.

So let's start by looking in the mirror with what sounds, on the face of it, like an existential question but is in fact a highly practical and important one:

How do I find out what I stand for?

What you stand for is not about your vision for the organization. Chances are there is already one in place that you need to buy into if you want to stay and whichever one is in place now is likely to change as events unfold. Instead, what you stand for needs to be something deeper which goes to the core of the value you bring to the world. It speaks to what is unique and true about you.

There are countless exercises available to help you discover your true self. Whether they involve choosing from a list of values or writing your own eulogy they all share one characteristic. They are all exercises that people like me get excited about and people like you are seldom keen to complete!

That being said it is true that discovering your true self and building deep self-awareness is a life long journey. The only way a few pages in a book on how to get an executive promotion can help is if they start you on that search in a way that enriches your prospects rather than derails your progress.

This search must be designed to help us answer the question "why on earth do you think you deserve to be an executive?".

The fact that you may have been around for a long time won't cut it as an answer. The fact that other people, who may be seemingly less qualified, have made the cut is a shame but not a reason. The fact that you are good at what you do is great but also another reason why you deserve to stay where you are.

Of course, you could argue that it would be enough to stand for whatever it is the people who are in charge of promotions stand for. The problem with this position is that unless the alignment is real, you will display what psychologists call "incongruent behaviors" i.e. you'll come across as a phony. And even if you manage to avoid these, there remains the fact that if all you do is sing from the same song sheet with the same voice as everyone else, your voice won't be heard and your presence at the executive table won't be required.

Knowing what you stand for helps you in two ways. It allows you to identify the core muscles that will enable you to balance the wobble board. It also makes clear the value that you can add to the executive team.

The two worst pieces of advice you may receive on your search for self-awareness are "just be yourself" and the so-called golden rule that you should "treat others the way you want to be treated". Jerks love these. They provide them with the perfect excuses for displaying their worst excesses and bullying others.

"Do unto others what you would like them to do unto you" is never a good idea for masochists! And "being yourself" takes many different forms depending on the circumstances. Our "family self" may well be different from our "work self". Our "intimate self" is not always the same as our "public self". That's not a bug; it's a feature of being a well-adjusted human being. What we need is for you to be the most skillful version of yourself.

Here are three steps to help you on your search for what you stand for.

1.   Introspection

You need to start by doing a bit of thinking on your own.

- **What are the traits that you exhibit across most circumstances?**
- **What are the elements of your biography that you find interesting, unusual, unique and valuable?**
- **What are your likes and dislikes in others and in you?**
- **What will you not compromise on?**

These questions will help you form a clearer picture of what you want to project to the world. The answers will also help you understand some of the non-negotiable, valuable or potentially destructive traits that you carry with you and which will make you a credible, authentic and impactful executive.

2.   Investigation

Unfortunately for some of us however, the way we think we are is not always the way others see us. Not all mirrors are as honest as Snow White's wicked queen's one! That's why other people's experience of us is a valuable source for adjusting our blurry perceptions. Go out and seek feedback.

- **How do you come across?**
- **What do other people value?**
- **What do they dislike?**

Don't go for some kind of 360-feedback exercise against a model. Just have a conversation with the people you trust to tell you the truth. Don't react. Don't object. Don't filter. Just listen carefully and thank them for their insights and honesty.

3.   Validation

Now bring the two together.

- **What are the crossovers between your introspection and investigation?**
- **What is the picture that is starting to emerge?**

A great way to do this is to try to come up with a phrase that marries both.

As an example, my mantra is "there must be a better way and together we can find it" which marries my desire always to challenge, my curiosity and my need to work with others, with the value they see in me of having deep rooted knowledge of my topic combined with an insatiable and somewhat irreverent need to question it.

It doesn't really matter if it's well articulated. No one but you needs to know what it is. You just have to make a first step in formulating something that you can test out. It simply needs to be something you can use to gauge your self-worth. It should be something that you can use to understand/predict how you are likely to respond. It should be something that describes you, to you.

There is a danger any time you conduct this kind of inquiry. The danger is that you become a caricature of yourself. You will have seen it when people use pseudo personality type instruments. They act out an even more extreme version of what they have been told they are.

STEP 3 – STEADFAST IMPACT

The other danger is that you try to create something that you think others want to hear. That would be a mistake. You are not writing an advert. This is not a mini CV. This is just about you becoming aware of your behavior so you can moderate your impact and respond appropriately to all your constituencies without having to compromise your truth. That is why having clear windows to look through in order to understand what others need is as critical as knowing what you can offer.

How do I know what my varied audiences need from me?

On the face of it this is a pretty easy challenge. All you have to do if you want to know what people need is ask and listen. However, things are never as easy as they first appear.

The challenge in asking is two-fold. Who do you ask? And what do you ask them about?

When it comes to "who do you ask?" your concern should be about filters. Our windows are always dirty. Every role comes with its own filters in terms of people you interact with. You need to mitigate for the resulting lack of breadth. Here are a couple of tips.

1. **Vary the people you ask.**

Go through your diary for the last few weeks and identify those you have interacted with the most. Is one of the wobble board constituencies missing (e.g. suppliers or the finance community)? What can you do to orchestrate more interactions with them? Can you get help from someone?

2. **Go beyond the squeaky wheels.**

The more senior you get, the more extremes you encounter. A CEO for example is much more likely to hear from customers who are insanely happy or ferociously annoyed than she is to come across normal customers whose only opinion of her organization is "it's ok". You have to shelter yourself from extremes.

The easiest way to do this is to elicit the contact yourself. Avoid focus groups. Pick up the phone. Have a conversation. Casually interact with people.

- **What do they need?**
- **What are they looking for from an organization like yours?**
- **Who is their supplier of choice?**

If "who do I ask" was our first challenge, then "what do I ask them about" is our second one. The key here is to be fully conscious that everybody lies. We lie to others and to ourselves. We lie for protection (whether it be to protect ourselves or others) and we lie for embellishment and exaggeration. So here is the next tip:

3. Remember that everybody lies

If you don't believe me when I say that everybody lies, next time you walk in the office first thing in the morning and someone asks you "how are you?" stop, look at them in the eyes and say "well, I am so glad you asked because actually I really need to talk to someone about an issue I'm facing…" and watch their reaction. Not only do we lie, but we expect to lie and be lied to.

The trick when finding out what people need is to go beyond the obvious (the first thing they think of) or the protective (the stuff they tell you about because it is easy). The best thing to do is start with a question that will generate a broad answer. Something like "when we are at our best and really meet your needs, what are we actually doing?" It is much harder to go for the obvious and easy when faced with a thoughtful and interesting question! So listen to the words but always dig deeper for the truth.

Of course, whatever you ask and however others respond will only be as good as whatever you hear and unfortunately, as senior people generally and leaders in particular, we are not very good at listening.

The biggest tip I can give you if you want to know what others need (which you must if you are to have an impact) is:

4.   Listen to understand, not to justify, answer or argue

Most executives in most meetings are not so much listening as reloading. They are rehearsing their next line of argument whilst you are still half-way through yours. It's a fun dance to observe but not a very productive process if you are to learn and understand what people need.

Yet, when you start to ask people what they need they will expect a response and you will feel the need to anticipate their question. Avoid thinking whilst you are listening. It is hard but not impossible. Think of yourself as a journalist just capturing the news with no filter or opinion. If you need to give a response, then formulate it after they have spoken. This will force you to pause which will make you seem and look even more interested which in turn will make them feel great!

Because they are mainly about thinking and listening, building self and social-awareness feels rather passive to many achievement-driven leaders. Don't disregard this however as it will determine the success of your impact.

At the root of Steadfast Impact lies our ability to be true to ourselves (having a honest mirror) whilst being able to impact the varied people around us by having a deep understanding of their needs (having clear windows).

Making Steadfast Impact work is about being able to vary your message in a way that resonates for different people without compromising your values and those of the organization, especially under pressure. At the risk of making this sound like a trailer for some kind of superhero chapter, we now need to work out how you will use your power.

RECAP

Whether you have an impact or not will depend on you (as the source of this impact) and the response from the people you are aiming to impact (i.e. the targets of your impact). What makes impact complex for executives is the sheer number of targets to impact as well as the huge variety of their demands and needs.

Having a Steadfast Impact requires you to master two variables – "mirror and windows".

The mirror stands for a deep understanding of what drives you and how this will help or hinder your impact, as well as a genuine understanding of what you stand for. The windows are the filters you apply to understanding others.

Having an honest mirror helps you answer the question "How do I find out what I stand for?"

There are three steps to answering this question.

- Introspection - searching for the crossovers between the different versions of yourself (e.g. public self, family etc.).
- Investigation - finding out how other people see you (e.g. seeking feedback and data).
- Validation - putting both together to create insights on what makes you valuable.

To make sure our windows are clear we need to ask, "How do I know what my varied audiences need from me?"

To answer this, you need to:

- Ask a variety of people whose opinion is neither extremely positive nor negative
- Listen to the words and dig for the truth
- Listen to understand, not to justify, answer, or argue

Knowing what you stand for and what people need is a precondition for Steadfast Impact.

14 POWER PLAYS – ADAPTING TO RESPOND WHILST STAYING AUTHENTIC TO BE STRONG

QUESTIONS THIS CHAPTER WILL ANSWER
How can I vary my message whilst remaining consistent?
How can I do this under intense pressure?

Forget authority and forget control: influence is the only tool you have to create value.

You cannot control the wobble board.

You cannot control what your staff think after a town hall meeting. You cannot control what parliamentarians do or journalists write after a government committee meeting in which you have given evidence. You cannot control the recommendations of a sell side analyst. You cannot control what customers tell others.

How they think and what they do is at their discretion.

If you're looking to control, then you do whatever it takes even if this means you have to vary what you stand for.

If you believe you have authority then you stick to your message even if this means your audience does what you want, despite knowing it is the wrong thing to do.

Being able to vary your message to influence your audience whilst remaining consistent in your aim is a habit good leaders have. To do so under intense pressure is one great executives master.

Let's take each in turn.

How can I vary my message whilst remaining consistent?

Varying your message is about impact and influence. Impact and influence is about power. When you understand where your power comes from and how it impacts others, you can vary your message (your influencing strategy) whilst remaining consistent in your aim (your truth).

There are two variables to power – the source of your power and its target.

When it comes to the target we have clarity. Your targets are the wobble board constituencies - your employees, customers and suppliers along with the finance community. We've already looked at how to discover what they want in our last chapter. We have no control over their needs, wants and desires.

The one variable you can control is you. What matters is what you see as the source of your power and how you decide to target this.

The most obvious answer to what is the source of your power is that you are. That would seem like a logical place to start. After all it is your experience, expertise and story that has brought you to a place where you can aspire to be a leader.

This being so, you would be surprised at how often leaders forget they are the source of their own power. I call this "my daddy is bigger than yours" power. Remember those times in playgrounds, wherever you are from, when you were stuck for somewhere to go with your argument? You would always go back to someone else as the source of your power. It was either my daddy is bigger than yours, or any other attributes you could assign to your carers that you felt made you somehow superior to the child you were arguing with.

Think about your own workplace. I am sure you too can identify "my daddy is bigger than yours" moments. Whether it is someone arguing their project is of strategic importance because the CEO mentioned it at the last all hands meeting or someone else pointing out that their boss, unlike yours is on the succession plan for CEO, we often find ourselves relying on someone else as the source of our power.

This is not a good place to start. It is a dependent rather than an assertive form of power. It is one that can disappear as quickly as the person you are dependent on.

Building effective power

Unfortunately, even once we abandon this dependence, we do tend to hang on to the idea that power is something we should have over someone. To this end, we approach any influencing strategy with the aim of making other people feel weaker/smaller than we do. We want them to be subservient to our will.

If that's your approach then the likelihood is you will use things that you have, rather than people you know, as the source of your power. You will replace my daddy is bigger than yours with my job is bigger than yours. My budget, knowledge, experience, car, house or success is bigger than yours. This is what psychologists call personalized power.

The problem with using this form of power is twofold. First personalized power begets personalized power. If you try to make me feel weaker I will do my best to fight back. Second, it's a problem because your focus will be on forcing your message, rather than adapting/selling it. The more you focus on you, the weaker your ability to impact.

By simply changing the focus of your power from you as the source, to others as the target, you can have a much better outcome.

The magic question

To achieve flexibility of approach whilst retaining consistency of message we need to think of power not as being about making someone else weaker and you superior but instead making them stronger and more capable.

A word of caution though, this is not the same as making them happy. If you are aiming to make your target happy then you will have to do and say whatever you need to do and say to succeed in this. That means you can't remain consistent in your messaging. Think about tough messages like redundancy plans or dividend cuts. The only way to make people happy is to do neither. You have to change the message.

The secret to a successful power interaction is to be able to answer in the affirmative the question: "have I made them feel stronger and more capable?"

This question forces you to focus on your target (it doesn't matter what you say if they don't feel stronger and more capable). It forces you to adapt to meet their needs. It also avoids you having to change the message. This is not about have I said what they want to hear, but rather, have I conveyed my message in a way that makes them stronger and more capable.

Get back to the redundancy/dividend cut example. You still have to give the message but what will you do to give your audience strength? Maybe you need to think about training to help them find new roles, maybe you need to think about your investor relations' strategy?

Think about being interviewed by an awkward parliamentarian posturing to their electorate (they exist) or an overzealous journalist trying to get ratings (there are some). Once you understand their needs there is a myriad of ways to pitch your message.

What will make that parliamentarian stronger and more capable? Maybe it is to show them the respect they need their constituents to see. Maybe it is to pitch your message with reference to jobs in their constituency?

How about that journalist? Maybe you can make their job easier by delivering a pithy quote. Maybe you need to think about how to shape your message in the most newsworthy way possible?

The key here is to think, "how do I make them feel stronger and more capable?" and the answer is always about "how do I help them balance their wobble board?"

Here are the things to keep in your mind when trying to apply this kind of power:
- Think of yourself as a doctor or teacher. What will make my patient/pupil stronger and more capable (if not necessarily happy).
- Remember that interactions should not be competitions. If you come out of an interaction feeling like you've won,

your counterparts probably feel they've lost - and that's not a desirable outcome.

- Others will only give you their discretionary effort if they see you as worthy of this which means they believe you to be authentic (consistent) as well as in their corner (flexible to their need.).
- If you lose your core you can't balance. Do not change your message; adapt it to others' needs.

How can I do this under intense pressure?

The problem with pressure is that it throws out all your good intentions. It makes you blind to the research you have conducted on what others need and diminishes your self-control. It makes all the tips above irrelevant.

Remember personalized power begets personalized power so as soon as your interlocutor makes you feel weaker, or as soon as you feel under attack, chances are you will fight back.

Don't!

Losing your self-control will simply turn the conversation into a drama. And trust me for each "my daddy is bigger than yours" example I have witnessed at work, I have been privy to tens of dramas.

In fact, psychotherapists have a helpful model that Stephen Karpman codified – it's known as the drama triangle. It is worth looking into if you want more detail but in its simplest form it identifies the three roles people take in conflict and which make up a drama.

First comes the Victim. This is the person who feels badly done to. They feel powerless and look for someone to save them. Every time you hear someone say "but they don't let me" or "I want to do this, but I don't have a budget" in your business, you have found a victim. When you are trying to influence someone, you may end up seeing yourself as a victim, maybe of circumstances, or of your interlocutor's intentions or stupidity.

For every victim we need a Persecutor – someone to whom blame can be ascribed. Being a persecutor is not about influence, but about control. It is about allocating fault.

The third character in our drama is the Rescuer. The rescuer seems like an appealing role as it looks at first sight like someone who is keen to help. However, we do well to remember that rescuers depend on victims for their existence, so their help can be short-lived and low impact. There are plenty of rescuers in business whose impact tends to stop at collusion.

What is so appealing about the drama triangle is that it perfectly describes our default position when influencing turns to conflict. It encapsulates the roles you are more likely to default to under stress when trying to influence.

Remember the types of power we discussed earlier. Becoming a persecutor means relying on personalized power. Being a victim is losing your power altogether in search of a rescuer you can depend on.

Breaking out of the triangle means changing your stance to an assertive one and one that will be generative rather than destructive. You need to be back on an equal and steady footing thinking, "have I made them feel stronger and more capable?"

There are many tricks and techniques communication

professionals use to help their clients avoid dramas. I am in awe of some of them and deeply frustrated by others. The problem with some media training is that it risks transforming a subset of people into automatons. You've seen them. Tell them it's a good question. Repeat the question. Answer the question you wanted them to ask rather than the one they asked and repeat your three points ad nauseum. The worst politicians are the best at this stuff.

That is not to say that some of the practices out there are all useless. Here are some of the ones a number of executives with whom we discussed Steadfast Impact have told us they value above all others. These tips will help you regain your composure and plan your impact so that it remains steadfast.

- **Know your audience.**

I know we covered this already in the last chapter, but it needs to be said again. This is not about knowing others' agendas, but about knowing them as people. Know their desires and their preoccupations. Influence is all about them and if you want to make them feel stronger and more capable you can never know enough.

- **Don't script the interaction, write down the outcome.**

When preparing for set pieces (a Q&A session with staff, a parliamentary inquiry, a Capital Markets Day or indeed an end of year review) I often see people writing down scripts. Sure, you should be prepared and of course you should rehearse the answers to the questions you are likely to be asked. What you shouldn't do though is try to script a conversation. Don't fall into the trap of scripting the interaction in advance. You may think your answers to everything are brilliant, but the truth is others will never exactly follow the flow of the arguments you have planned. The only reason they might is if you drag them along with these and that would be a sure way to lose impact. Instead of scripting the flow, ensure you are clear on your message and how you can phrase this in a way that resonates.

- **Recognize the triggers.**

We all have triggers. They can be triggers that indicate we are getting nervous (and therefore more likely to lose our self-control) like sweaty palms or shaking legs. Or they can be what poker players call "tells", the signals we give unconsciously that we are uncomfortable or bluffing. You need to know yours so that you can avoid going down the path they lead you along. Replay some situations in your mind that did not go well to find out what the triggers might have been. Ask colleagues you trust what your "tells" might be by contrasting the difference between when they have seen you at your best and when they have witnessed times where you didn't impact as effectively.

- **Pause to reflect.**

Pausing is the best way to maintain your composure. The more under pressure we are to come up with answers the quicker we tend to want to respond (and incidentally the faster we end up speaking). It's a mistake. Pausing doesn't make you look unsure, it makes you look thoughtful. Pausing makes the other person feel valued, as you seem to consider their question important enough to want to give the best possible answer. Use pauses to reflect on what has been asked and how it fits your message.

You will only be able to have Steadfast Impact if your aim is to make other people feel stronger and more capable. This will ensure you are authentic by keeping to your truth whilst being adaptable enough to have an impact. The more stress you are under, the more difficult it is going to be but by keeping in mind that your role as an executive is to release your wobble board's constituencies' discretionary effort to create the value you seek you will avoid the dramas that come from poor Steadfast Impact.

Talking about dramas, if Shakespeare (or indeed Voltaire) were alive today they would find top team meetings a rich seam to mine for inspiration. Knowing when and how to contribute as well as manage yourself and others in an executive team is the final area of Steadfast Impact and indeed the final area of making the transition to executive we need to cover. Let's do this next before we set out your week one game plan for making the transition.

RECAP

Your ability to impact and influence those around you (i.e. your power) is your lever to create value.

Given all your wobble board constituencies have different needs you will need to influence them in different ways. However, you have to remain consistent (authentic) if you are to be a trusted interlocutor.

The key to managing both flexibility and consistency is to understand the nature of power.

The two strategies that ensure failure are:

- Try to make them happy (i.e. you say anything they might want to hear)
- Try to make them small (i.e. you try to have power over them)

The only strategy that ensures success is if you try to make others feel stronger and more capable. This ensures that you as the source of power stick to your message (consistency) whilst at the same time targeting your impact to others' needs (flexibility) so they release their discretionary effort.

The key to success is to ask yourself constantly "have I made this person feel stronger and more capable?"

This is however hard to do under pressure when your reflexes come into play and you default to habits. Our main habits resemble a drama triangle where we adopt the roles of victim (how dare they say this), persecutor (I'll show them how wrong they are) or rescuer (oh dear, let me get them out of this hole).

Developing new habits to cope with these circumstances is important. Here are some things to keep in mind:

- Know your audience
  Intimately. Know what their desires and fears are. The more you know them as people the less you will see them as the roles they play.

- Don't script the interaction, write down the outcome
  In set pieces, don't fall into the trap of scripting the interaction in advance. Instead be clear on your message and focus on your audience.

- Recognize the triggers.
  Whether yours are sweaty palms, shaking legs or something else altogether, we all have "tells." Know yours.

- Pause to reflect
  Pausing doesn't make you look unsure – it makes you look thoughtful. Use pauses to reflect on what has been asked and how your response can reinforce your message.

15 THE 3 LIKES TEST FOR MAKING TEAMS WORK

QUESTIONS THIS CHAPTER WILL ANSWER
How do I know the value I bring to the executive table?
When and how should I contribute for maximum impact?

Executive teams are like families – you almost never get to choose yours.

Even CEOs don't always have that much room for maneuver. There are plenty of reasons why they might have to appoint, or keep, someone on their team.

Just like families, executive teams are inherently seemingly dysfunctional. Team members argue. They don't necessarily like each other. They jockey for position and fight for budgets as well as attention. There are preferences and feuds.

They can be especially difficult for those not born into them. Becoming a new member of an executive team is often both intimating and uncomfortable. It's like gaining a new family through marriage – you have to quickly find your voice, but also use this at the right time in a way that lands rather than alienates.

Many executives we interviewed talked about the discomfort they experienced early on around the executive table. They described being unsure of the value they brought to the table (beyond their immediate functional expertise). They talked about their hesitancy in making points, especially when they fundamentally disagreed with others.

There is one thing they all agreed on though. Having an impact around the executive table may be harder than doing so in other settings but the mechanics are the same as anywhere else. Having Steadfast Impact is still about mirror and windows.

To be a credible voice that others listen to is fundamentally about being clear about the value you bring and being savvy in judging your audience.

How do I know the value I bring to the table?

You would think most executives should be pretty clear on the value they bring to the table by the time they are asked to sit at it. You would be wrong. The problem is that you think you know the value you bring, but that may not be the value others see.

They are hundreds of reasons why you may have been appointed. The CEO may see you bringing a different way of thinking, a different perspective, some knowledge that others lack or even simply as a new voice. That may be entirely different from what you think gives you the right to be there.

The truth is that we all have a fairly restricted view of our value at work (after all, aren't we forever told that we should be able to fit this into a two-page CV). By the time you reach an executive position you need to be well aware that you are not what, or whom, you know.

Here are some points you should consider in order to understand the value you bring to the team. By working through each of them you will be much clearer about the nature of the contributions you make that will bring value to others.

- **Why were you brought in?**

Chances are no one will ever tell you unless you ask. Of course, they will tell you that you are a worthy addition to the team. They will let you know what they think of the results you deliver, your experience, your expertise and any number of other attributes. What they will forget to tell you though is how you fit in. What is your value on the team? So, make sure you ask.

By knowing how you fit in you will gain your license to impact.

Don't become a caricature of the role you think you have been given however. Your fit gives you your license. How you use this is up to you. Don't be restricted by what others want if you know there is more you can contribute. This takes us to the second point.

- **You are more than what you know.**

There are literally millions of highly competent HR professionals, excellent IT experts and outstanding sales people. The fact that you know your trade got you to where you are today, but it does not define you. You need to think about your value in a far broader sense.

Knowing the value you can bring will ensure you don't end up just playing to a role you have been assigned. It will also make you confident in your ability to contribute. That being said you will need to ensure that, whenever you add value beyond what you understand your brief to be, you tackle the next point.

- **Have you got back up?**

You are not only entitled to your opinions, you are obliged to have some. If you don't have an opinion on everything that is being discussed, you need to find one pretty quickly.

Often though you will be expected to have an opinion on something that lies outside your natural zone of operations. Sometimes you may feel that, despite the fact you have not been asked your opinion, you want to voice one. Both are ok as long as you can back up what you say.

Backing up your opinion comes in two forms – facts and stories. Don't believe that the facts speak for themselves. They never do. What makes other executives accept facts is when they are backed up with stories – especially stories from the middle of the organization. Remember what we said before? The more you can help other executive team members learn what the organization truly looks like, the more they will buy your point.

If you can't back up your opinion with facts and stories you will need to get back up from other team members. The best way to get this is by tackling the next point.

- **What is your intent?**

Why do you want to say what you are about to say?

If people do not understand your intent they will ascribe one to you. The problem is that, due to the paranoid nature of executive team members, the intent they will ascribe is always the worst.

Make sure you always make your intent clear. If you don't believe me just start a sentence with "the reason I am saying this is …" and watch the relief on your colleagues' faces as they realize they won't have to ascribe an intent to your intervention.

They may still doubt you though so never just stick to a once-only declaration of your intent. The more contentious your point, the more times you will need to explain why you believe it is important to make it.

For the avoidance of doubt let me repeat something. At the root of Steadfast Impact lies the question "have I made them feel stronger or more capable?" So, if your answer to "why do I want to say this" is that it will allow you to grandstand, score points, fight back, belittle colleagues or a combination of the four, then don't say it. It's not worth your while, it will diminish your immediate impact and your long-term standing.

When I observe an executive team I normally make a simple diagram of the table on a piece of paper and draw arrows that go from the person who speaks, to the person who listens. Most of the time, by the end of the meeting, my diagrams are pretty one-dimensional - a lot of arrows go back and forth from executives to the chairperson. With the best functioning teams this diagram is a mess with arrows going back and forth all over the place. What is rather consistent though for all teams is the number of arrows that land in the middle of the table.

Whether they are points made for posturing or interventions that are badly timed or constructed, these arrows underscore the second important dimension of impact in an executive team. The value you think you bring, or that others tell you you bring, is only realized if your impact lands on the people around the table, rather than on the table itself!

That means that you need to make and time your impact perfectly.

When and how should I contribute for maximum impact?

Don't you just love a good team development event? There is something cathartic about running together in the mud, or hugging a tree, or any number of other activities you would never choose to conduct in your private life but have to suffer for the sake of your job!

Now here is the good news. Knowing when and how to impact in the team does not require you to have forged deep and meaningful relationships with your colleagues at the top of some mountain. As we saw all the way back in chapter 5 though, when we looked at the relationships to results pyramid, you do need to have great working relationships.

Great working relationships mean that you need to understand the people you work with and the way they work to deliver results.

When we were discussing the best way to have an impact in an executive team, one of our interviewees shared with us a simple model he uses to think through the dynamics of a situation. We call this the "3 likes" test.

When thinking about having an impact in a conversation you should ask yourself three questions:
- Do I like the person?
- Do I like the way they work?
- Do I like the results they get?

This may seem like a weird set of questions to ask but the answers reveal some pretty interesting strategies when it comes to the timing and tone of your intervention. Let's take each variable in turn.

Do I like the person?

Liking the person is great. It's nice to have people around us who we like.

If you like someone you may support them more, give them time to develop themselves or their point. That's great.

But liking them is not a condition for success. In fact, if you like a person you may spend too much time trying to cover for them. You may become a rescuer when they shouldn't be a victim.

Thinking about the relationship you have with the person will enable you to think through the filters you apply to their contribution.

Do I like the way they work?

You can compromise on value but never on values. Do you like the way they work is an important question. It talks to the "how" of what is achieved. It comes before the results question because it is more important.

The question "Do I like the way they work?" is targeted to highlight the sustainability of the results you get.

Now you may not like the way they work because you don't understand it or it doesn't fit with your mental models. It may not be anything to do with them being untrustworthy. In fact, we ask "do I like the person" first in order to understand what may be clouding your judgment.

But if you ever find yourself thinking, "I don't like the way they work" you know you have an intervention to make. As an executive you want to be known and remembered for what you contributed, not what you tolerated.

Do I like the results they get?

The reason this is the last question and not the first is because everyone likes great results. Your life as an executive will be focused on corrective actions to assure their delivery. If we were to start with this question and you answered yes to it, you would seldom spend much time considering the rest.

As we have seen though, by asking do I like the person and the way they work first, we discover something important about their results we may not have previously considered.

If you don't like the person nor their results, but you like the way they work, then you need to get over your dislike of them and guide them or be patient.

If you like the person, but don't like the way they work and don't like the results they get, then do something even if it hurts.

Whether or not you like the person, if you like the results they get but don't like the way they work, this is tough but you're going to have to call it.

If you like all three then relax and celebrate. Your only intervention should be congratulatory. In this situation though, you need to be cautious of avoiding complacency.

Results are important, but they are lag, not lead, indicators. When judging when and where to impact, your job is to ensure you are ahead of results.

Incidentally this is a tool you can apply now irrespective of your current position. It is a great tool to use before you discuss development options with those who report to you. It is also a great one to think through when you are making new appointments. Using it from today will additionally help you develop your Steadfast Impact muscles. The more intuitive you become in your use of the tool, the more intuitive you will be in gauging when and how to impact.

Now what?

So, here we are. I have now told you everything we discovered on our search in how to fast track your transition to executive. I have told you about the three unique characteristics of executive roles – Boundless Perspective, Vertical Agility and Steadfast Impact. I have shared with you some ideas, perspectives, models and tools to aid you in your transition. At this stage I should probably wish you good luck and leave you to digest the lot but there is one more thing we need to do before I let you go. I partly need to sound a note of caution, but mainly I need to help you put all this to work.

The fact is I have enough self-awareness and experience to know that people have great intentions whenever they think about their development but are frequently pretty terrible at actually putting things into practice. They either try too hard, too quickly or more usually do very little. After all, the moment you put this book down you will be inundated by a myriad of things to do. Before I go I would like to share with you a game plan for starting your journey now!

RECAP

Executive teams are often dysfunctional by nature. Having an impact on the team is about power and, as we know, at the root of effective power lies an understanding of our value along with our ability to flex our impact upon the target.

The dynamic of power in executive teams is the same as in any other setting — mirror and windows! You must know your value and know your audience. Only then can you be clear on the what, the when and the how of your interventions.

How to determine your value

Here is a set of pointers to help you discover the value you bring to the executive table:

- Why were you brought in?
  You must ask. Don't just ask what they saw in you as an individual but more importantly what they see you bring to the team (i.e. how you fit in).

- You are more than what you know.
  Your CV got you so far, but it is your story that will differentiate you. You are not your experience but the lessons you have drawn from it. These are unique to you.

- Have you got back up?
  You are not only entitled to your opinions: you are obliged to have some. That being said the further you go from what you know, the more facts and stories you will need to back up what you assert.

- What is your intent?
  If people do not understand your intent they will ascribe one to you. Make sure they ascribe the right one by telling them what it is!

How to know your team

Knowing your team in this context is about understanding the filters you apply to the judgments you make. When thinking about any intervention you wish to make, ask yourself:

- Do I like the person?
  This will tell you if you are intervening to score a point or help you gauge your capacity for support.

- Do I like the way they work?
  This will help you determine the value you can bring or the stand you must take.

- Do I like the results they get?
  This will help you focus your impact on both value and values.

The answers to all three questions will help you clarify the reason for your intervention and guide you towards making it in the right way.

Being clear now about your value and using the "three likes" test with your current team you will help you build your Steadfast Impact muscle.

16 THE WEEK ONE GAME PLAN

In the United Kingdom they say the Queen thinks the country smells of fresh paint because wherever she goes has been freshly repainted. The same is true for leaders. It is hard for them to know what their organization truly smells like. Managers see it as their role to protect them from the ugly realities of work. Management by wandering around is a great leadership practice, but it only works if you can avoid the blindfold that colleagues are keen to ensure you wear.

Over a decade ago, a CEO I was consulting with, aware of the impact of his role on his team's ability to speak freely, asked me to conduct a simple exercise. Could I go around and interview his direct reports to get some feedback and insights from them on what he could do better[13].

To his credit, there was very little they were saying to me that they had not previously told him to his face - they were at pains to explain that actually he was probably the executive most open to feedback they had ever worked for. In fact, in the middle of one of these conversations, my interviewee asked, "what exactly does he want to know as I have never felt I couldn't give him the feedback he sought?" I went on to explain that there was one particular behavior the CEO had been trying to work on

---

13. As an aside it is common to ask people like me for feedback on what you could do better rather than feedback on what you do well. Whilst it is both honorable and worthwhile to want to better yourself I am always at pains to remind clients that you can never excel unless you know what you do well, so you can keep replicating this.

and that he wanted to gauge how effective he had been in his endeavor.

The answer I got offers a worthwhile caution as you embark on your personal journey of attaining the outcome you seek. "Ah so that's what he has been trying to do. Now I get it. We all thought he had gone a bit weird over the last few months!"

My key message as we come towards the end of our time together could be, as I alluded to in chapter 3, "don't be weird", but let me borrow a much better phrase to make the same point, "first, do no harm."

Let's face it, we've all been there. Armed with new-found courage and ideas we decide that we are going to make some big improvements in our lives. We know we can change and we're going to get on with it. We will stop smoking, drinking and eating chocolate. We can even do all three on the same day if we put our minds to it. Millions of people do this at the beginning of the year. Diet books fly off the shelves. The fact that diet books fly off the shelves year after year should give you a clue as to the rate of success of these resolutions.

So, first do no harm.

Please don't rush out and try to practice everything I have advocated in these pages at once. Don't make a resolution to be an executive by the end of this week. It won't work. They'll just think you've gone weird.

Let me share with you a simple formula that will ensure you are much more likely to succeed if you start after one week. This first week will be about working through it.

The change equation

$D \times V \times P > C$

This equation contains the variables that need to be tackled for successful change to happen. You might have come across other variations of it and if they work for you do feel free to use them but if you haven't, here is how it works.

The D stands for Dissatisfaction. No change will ever occur if you are delighted with your status quo. You need to be dissatisfied about something if you are to commit to change.

The V is for Vision. Have you envisaged what it will be like when you achieve your goal? How will your life be different? Having no vision of where you want to go makes it hard to get there. Having a poorly articulated one makes it difficult to recognize you have arrived.

The P is for Practical steps or Plan. If you don't know what you have to do it will be difficult to do it.

Note that there is a multiplier between each of the variables. They are not additive. If one is overlooked, then the rest of them add up to nothing.

Finally, the combined value of the three elements above must outweigh the cost (C) of the change you seek to make. The math does matter here. This is not a greater than/equals sign but a greater than sign. What is the point of making the effort to change if it will cost you more, or as much as it will bring?

To succeed in achieving the top leadership position you seek, you must work through the equation. This is what the game plan is for week one.

Here is how it works in practice.

Make four columns on a piece of paper (one for each of the equation's variables). We are going to use the first four days of the week to explore each in turn.

Monday – Tackling the D

It is interesting how many people climb the organizational hierarchy for no other reason than they think it is what is expected of them. It is also surprising how many people end up in leadership positions because of the need on the part of the organization to promote them to keep them rather than a need on their part to accept the call to lead.

The problem with making a change either because we think we ought to or because we aim to please/impress other people is that it is unlikely to succeed. What will actually keep you on your development path is the desire never to experience your dissatisfaction again. If you can use the negative energy of dissatisfaction and turn it into the positive force of desire, you will be on your way to success.

So today ask yourself the following question:

• **Why do I want to do this?**

Below are some supplementary questions you may want to think about to help inform your answer. There is no response that is right or wrong, or better or worse. Your answer is your answer. Do not feel guilty about it. All you have to do is to own your answer, as it is this sense of avoiding dissatisfaction or fulfilling a desire that will give you the resilience to reach your goal.

- What is it in your life right now that you are so unhappy about that you feel you need a new role?
- What is it that is driving your desire to change?
- Is this about you or fundamentally about someone else (a parent you are still trying to impress, or a partner you want to please)?
- Is becoming an executive the only course available to you to reach your goal?

Write down your thoughts in the D column. I know you're a high achiever but don't rush trying to complete all the columns in one day. Trust me when I say that you are not wasting your time – this needs to be a reflective, iterative process. You may well change your mind throughout the course of the day or even feel you want to add something later on in the week.

Your answers don't have to be well articulated. No one is going to check your work. Just be honest with yourself and make sure you keep a record of your thoughts.

Tuesday – Tackling the V

Having thought about your dissatisfaction and desire to seek a new position we come to the idea of Vision. Vision here is not the same as desire nor is it some grand design. What I mean by vision is simply whether you have thought about what your life will be like when you reach your goal.

If you have ever booked a holiday on the basis of the pictures you have seen in a brochure, you will know that sometimes it is worth checking out the reviews and a few other sources before you hand over your money!

The question we are looking to tackle here is

- **Do I truly know what I am getting myself into?**

Here are some of the avenues you may want to explore. Again, record your thoughts on your piece of paper as you not only may want to refer to them when the going gets tough but also refine them as you get more information.

- What will you be doing during your week?
- What will be different practically?
- What adjustments will you have to make to your current lifestyle?
- Can you picture what your environment will look like?
- Will you have to make any trade-offs?

To be useful your vision needs to be as clear and detailed as possible. "Everything will be great" or "I will have a great office" is not good enough. When people try to stop smoking they are often asked "what will you do after your evening meal instead of going out for a cigarette?" or, "what will you say to your friends when they ask if you are coming out for a smoke?" This is the level of detail you need to get into to make sure you know the extent of the differences between your current state and your goal state.

Wednesday – Tackling the P

Hopefully you will have found this book to be practical. So, it will help you determine the practical steps you need to take. If this is the case, then let's use the time we have today to make a Plan.

Whether you use SMART goals or other mechanism doesn't matter but use something to make sure you have a robust plan by the end of the day.

There are three questions that should form the basis of your plan.

- Which of the executive practices from the book can I integrate into my daily routines?
- What new activities will I have to undertake in order to embrace the remaining practices I couldn't include within what I already do?
- How am I going to go about doing both?

We should now have some pretty robust insights on the left-hand side of the equation. We should know what will drive you forward and what could potentially derail your progress. There is only one part of the equation left for us to complete tomorrow.

Thursday – Tackling the C

The cost of change is something we all feel when we experience it but seldom think about when we embark on a journey. I don't mean the cost by way of cash. We're pretty good at thinking about that one! I mean the psychological cost of change. I mean the impact change has on us as well as on those around us. If we don't think about it before we embark on our change effort, we may well have to pay the price when it is too late to do much about it.

So here is the question to reflect on today:

- **What will it cost you to seek and be appointed to the top leadership role you want?**

There are two sides to the cost variable you should consider.

The first refers to the costs of getting the executive role you want. You may have to leave some friendships behind. You may not be able to collude with some colleagues the way you have been used to doing. You may also have to spend more time at work, which may be costly at home. You may find yourself having to make choices and trade-offs between the things you have to do today for your team and the things you want to do for your organization tomorrow. These costs have always been present in some ways but your stated aim to become an executive will bring them even more into focus.

There will also be some costs when you get the role. There will be some obvious ones. Maybe you will have to move to some headquarters office somewhere. And there will be some less obvious ones. Maybe some people may look at you differently. Some of these costs will appear trivial whilst others will be huge. Whatever they are, you will have to meet them head on.

Try not to wear rose tinted glasses for this exercise. You may need to observe, or talk to, executives to identify the costs they have had to face.

You should never ignore this part of the equation as an absence of level-headedness and clear thinking about costs is what derails most change efforts. It is also a lot better to think about potential costs before you have had to incur them than to regret your decision after you have had to make payment.

Again, be as detailed as possible in your record keeping.

So, what are we going to do with our last working day?

Friday — Reviewing the equation

I know it may feel like overkill and you may be getting pretty sick of this equation by now but today is about looking at your insights in the round.

This equation is a bit like a masterpiece in an exhibition. You can look up close at the painting and see some really interesting details – a special stroke, a flash of color. But it is only when you take a couple of steps back that the overall picture is revealed.

Have a look across your columns. What do you see? Is a pattern emerging? Are you sure you have everything you need? Could there be another way of achieving your vision without having to incur the costs? Can some of the costs be avoided if we make the vision different or change the plan slightly?

I've said before that I like to think of the brain as a puddle of water on the ground. If you jump in the puddle the water becomes murky. If you step back and leave the puddle alone for a while everything becomes clear again. This book, and the last week of work on the equation, has been about jumping in the puddle. Today (and indeed this coming weekend) is about letting the water become clear again!

By the time you get to work next week I hope you will have a much clearer picture of where you want to go (or confirmation that your original picture was right all along), plus a practical plan, complete with workable practices, to get you to where you want to be.

Unlike with the rest of the book where we adopted the singular for ease of reading, we hope you will allow us to go back to the plural voice for this last sentence, as we both want to wish you well on your journey to getting the role you seek and making the difference you want to make.

RECAP

You may want to start your first week after reading this book by immediately implementing some of the tactics and ideas you have read about. Don't! It's normal for you to feel this way: you are a successful and driven leader. What is more important than starting the journey though is to make sure you know why you are undertaking it so as to be resilient when setbacks and pressures invariably crop up. Start this first week by working through a simple equation that ensures successful change. Your dissatisfaction, times your vision, times the practical steps you will take must be greater than the costs you will incur in unleashing the leader you know you can be. Travel well.

THE WINNING QUESTION SET

Whilst our research helped us highlight a relatively small number of unique characteristics of leadership roles it also generated a lot of techniques, models and tactics executives use to navigate them successfully. For anyone aspiring to win a top leadership position this can be somewhat overwhelming.

For this reason, we thought it might be a good idea by way of closing to extract, from everything we have covered, a number of key questions you should keep in your mind as you navigate your career.

We have organized them under the headings why, where and how. The job of a leader and especially an executive leader is to give hope and hope is not some sort of woolly ephemeral concept. Hope is simply the articulation of a goal (why), a will (what) and a way (how). By summarizing the habits we have covered as a set of questions we hope you will be able to focus your impact on delivering a compelling reason for people to follow you.

Why questions

1. Why do we do what we do?
2. Why do we have a right to exist?

What questions

3. What is the nature of my task?
4. What capabilities do we have?
5. What capabilities will we need?

How questions

6. How do I create value for the enterprise?
7. How do I increase collaboration in the enterprise?

8. How can we use what we do today to develop the capabilities we will need tomorrow?
9. How can I make others feel stronger and more capable?

And by way of a final thought, the fundamental question to keep at the back of your mind at all times is:

10. Why am I doing this?

Emmanuel Gobillot is the founder of Emmanuel Gobillot Limited, a boutique consultancy dedicated to leadership and organizational development services. The author of a number of business books including *'The Connected Leader'*, *'Leadershift'* and *'Follow The Leader'*, Emmanuel teamed up with Urbane Publications to unveil *'Disciplined Collaboration – Four Steps To Collaborative Success'* in 2016.

In a career spanning roles as consultant, HR director, Non-Executive Director and entrepreneur, **Katherine Thomas** has merged her psychology and accountancy expertise to help senior executives deliver breakthrough results through people and purpose. She is Co-founder and Managing Director of 'Collaboration Partners', a consultancy specializing in helping leaders and organisations develop effective collaboration. *Unleash your Leader* is her first book.

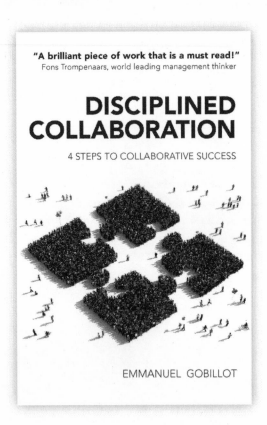

"A brilliant piece of work that is a must read!"
Fons Trompenaars, world leading management thinker

DISCIPLINED COLLABORATION

4 STEPS TO COLLABORATIVE SUCCESS

EMMANUEL GOBILLOT

'Working with and reading Emmanuel's work you realize that there is little in the market that goes beyond his concepts and practice of collaboration! A brilliant piece of work that is a must read!'

Fons Trompenaars, Thinkers50 and Business magazine top management thinker and author of Global phenomenon Riding the Waves of Culture

In this engaging, thoughtful and well-researched book, global speaker, consultant and leadership expert, Emmanuel Gobillot, identifies the real barriers to collaboration and proposes a disciplined approach to removing them. Combining the latest psychological and organisational research with pragmatic real-world application, *Disciplined Collaboration* shows you how to make your divisions add up again. This book will help you:

- Diagnose the issues that get in the way of collaboration in your organisation.
- Discover how to master the changing nature of influence from competition to collaboration.
- Learn how to deploy the 4 disciplines that will remove the fears of collaboration in your team.
- Find practical tools to help you reconnect individuals and teams.
- Be inspired by stories drawn from a breathtaking number of fields from business to history to medicine via tailoring and comedy!

Urbane
BUSINESS

Urbane Publications is dedicated to
developing and publishing
books that challenge, educate and fascinate.

From trade reference titles to
professional business books,
our goal is to publish what
YOU want to read.
Find out more at

Find out more at
urbanepublications.com